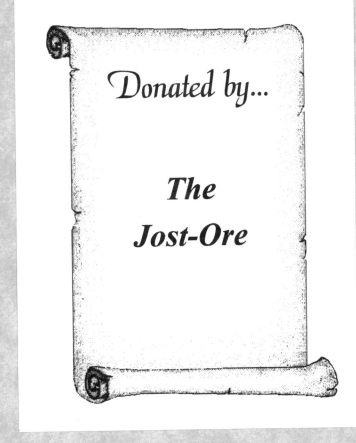

E.F. Jost
Columbus
11/21/95

Christmas '45:
Victory —
the best present,
and past,
of the century

VICTORY

Written and Compiled by Nancy J. Skarmeas

"We have to remember
that in the future
we will want to keep before our children
what this war was really like.
It is so easy to forget;
and then, for the younger generation,
the heroism and the glamour remain,
while the dirt, the hardships,
the horror of death
and the sorrow fade somewhat
from their consciousness."

Eleanor Roosevelt

IDEALS PUBLICATIONS INCORPORATED
Nashville, Tennessee

On the Cover
UNITED STATES MARINE CORPS WAR MEMORIAL
Photo by H. Armstrong Roberts

Copy Editor, Michelle Prater Burke
Electronic Prepress and Layout, Amilyn Lanning
Military Advisor, Julie D. Shively, Captain, USAF

ISBN 0-8249-4068-7

Printed and bound in the United States of America

Published by Ideals Publications Incorporated
535 Metroplex Drive, Suite 250
Nashville, TN 37211

Film separations by Precision Color Graphics, New Berlin, WI
Printed and Bound by Inland Press, Milwaukee, WI

PREFACE

Victory is published in commemoration of the fiftieth anniversary of the end of World War II. It is intended as a nostalgic look at the era, a scrapbook of American experience in wartime assembled from an eclectic collection of photographs, personal reminiscences, and accompanying factual information. Whereas we have made every effort to be accurate in the recording of facts, we present this book as neither a chronological, comprehensive historical textbook nor an all-inclusive military history of World War II. By necessity and by its very nature, *Victory* is a limited sampling of the people, the places, the images, and the moods of World War II, as seen through American eyes.

American life changed in almost every aspect during the war years. Between 1941 and 1945, the American people pulled together as never before in support of the Allied fight for freedom. Young men and women volunteered in record numbers for military service and, along with those drafted, served with pride and honor. Families accepted rationing, collected scrap metal, and put their savings into war bonds. Women who had never before worked outside their homes stepped forward to fill the jobs left empty by men gone to war. The leaders of industry answered the president's call and converted their plants to meet the demands of war production. In the armed services and on the home front, in every corner of American life, sacrifice was commonplace and heroism in abundant supply. It is this heroism and the American willingness to work together for a common cause that we remember in *Victory*.

General Dwight D. Eisenhower once said, "I hate war as only a soldier who has lived it can, only as one who has seen its brutality, its futility, its stupidity." We must all take his words to heart. War, at its core, is an evil to be avoided, and World War II brought suffering to millions of innocent people across the globe. But war is not to be avoided at all costs, not at the cost of the freedom and dignity and human rights of innocent people; aggression, repression, and terror cannot go unanswered in a free and civilized world. The American men and women who fought in the battles of World War II, and those at home who made the small daily sacrifices that added up to one of the most potent national civilian war efforts of all time, did so in defense of their way of life, and in the name of freedom. In *Victory* we remember the very transformation of American society brought on by the war years, and we honor the efforts of all Americans during World War II. In so doing, we also remember the cause for which we fought and honor the millions of citizens of the world who lost their lives in the Second World War.

"THE GREAT ARSENAL OF DEMOCRACY"
President Roosevelt, December 29, 1940.

On May 26, 1940, with much of the rest of the world at war, President Franklin Delano Roosevelt appealed to the pride and patriotism of the American people as he called on them to help build the nation's defenses. "While our Navy and our airplanes and our guns may be our first lines of defense," the president told his radio audience that night, "it is still clear that way down at the bottom, underlying them all, giving them their strength and sustenance and power, are the spirit and morale of a free people." Although it took the shocking attack on Pearl Harbor to fully mobilize the nation to the president's call, once inspired, the citizens on the home front proved as committed to the fight as the soldiers on the battlefields. American society was transformed. Factories stopped turning out automobiles and started producing tanks, planes, and guns. Families left their hometowns in record numbers to fill jobs in war plants in faraway cities. Business leaders put their skills to work for the government. And perhaps most significantly, women, more than three million of them, added welding and riveting and assembly-line work to their traditional chores of homemaking. American war production became the envy and the salvation of the world. In the words of a proud president, "The production which has flowed from this country to all the battlefields of the world has been due to the efforts of American business, American labor, and American farmers working as a patriotic team."

WESTERN AIRCRAFT PLANT—This new transport plane carries one of the greatest human or cargo loads of any plane now in mass production. It is built at a western aircraft plant equipped with the best and most modern air conditioning and fluorescent lighting systems in the country. *Photo Office of War Information, Courtesy National Archives.*

In his State of the Union address on January 6, 1942, President Roosevelt tried to rouse the industrial might of the nation. "The militarists of Berlin and Tokyo started the war," he declared, "but the massed, angered forces of common humanity will finish it." Using figures purposely inflated to inspire the full commitment of businesses, laborers, and every citizen, Roosevelt called upon American industry to produce 60,000 planes, 45,000 tanks, and 20,000 antiaircraft guns per year.

The attack on Pearl Harbor found the American naval fleet outnumbered and outdated. Roosevelt turned to Henry J. Kaiser, a sixty-year-old industrialist and entrepreneur, for help. Kaiser responded with the Liberty Ship. On January 20, 1942, the first Kaiser shipyard opened in Richmond, California. Hiring inexperienced but energetic workers, Kaiser produced ships in record time—sixty days from start to launch. In one 212 day period, 247 Liberty Ships were launched. The ships were slow in the water and sacrificed quality to quantity, but they carried supplies to the world's battlefields at a large enough volume to compensate for their occasional failure. Kaiser's success inspired the rest of the U.S. shipping industry to match his performance.

MANITOWOC, WISCONSIN—The USS *Robalo*, built by the Manitowoc Shipbuilding Company, is launched on May 9, 1943—another example of the continuing effort to provide ships for our fighting Navy. *Photo Courtesy National Archives.*

U.S. ARMY ORDNANCE DEPARTMENT ARSENAL— Women employees are turning out powder bags in the sewing room of an ordnance arsenal. Women workers perform all the bag cutting and sewing operations and load the bags with smokeless powder. *Photo U.S. Army Signal Corps, Courtesy National Archives.*

GRUMMAN AIRCRAFT ENGINEERING CORPORATION—Women production aids provide the final touches on outfitting one of the newest aircraft soon to be deployed to Europe. *Photo Courtesy National Archives.*

A newspaper columnist reported that for American women during World War II, "slacks became the badge of honor." With labor shortages holding up production at war plants throughout the U.S., women stepped in to fill positions once held exclusively by men. By 1944, 3.5 million American women were working on assembly lines—"Rosie the Riveter" was a fact of life across the U.S. After the war, many women returned to their prewar lives and roles, but never again would the American workplace be the sole domain of the male population.

America's war production boom not only changed the course of the war, it changed the very structure of American society. After years of depression and stagnation in the economy, war plant jobs enabled people to work again and sent families on the move. Rural Americans flocked to the cities; many moved west, where jobs were more plentiful. The face of the work force also began to change. The war years found blacks and women working alongside the white men who had previously dominated the workplace. In factories and shipyards across the nation, gender stereotypes and racial prejudices were challenged as every able hand was put to work.

KAISER SHIPYARDS, RICHMOND, CALIFORNIA—Women war workers play an important part in the construction of the Liberty Ship SS *George Washington Carver,* launched May 7, 1943. *Photo Office of War Information, Courtesy National Archives.*

PRESIDENT FRANKLIN D. ROOSEVELT

Franklin Delano Roosevelt served as president of the United States for twelve years and forty days. Four times the American people elected him as their leader. In fact, so long did Roosevelt inhabit the White House, and so full of crises and change were his years there, that when he died on April 12, 1945, a journalist remarked that it felt as if "history itself had died." Roosevelt was a master politician with a keen understanding of the power of public opinion. He knew that America's greatest asset in the war was its people, and he was ever aware of the need for their support for him and his policies. He also understood that America would have to depend upon and support the Allies if the war were to be won. A man with no military experience, Roosevelt filled the role of commander in chief during World War II with confidence, intelligence, and commitment.

QUEBEC CITY, CANADA— Prime Minister Winston Churchill, President Franklin D. Roosevelt, and Canadian Prime Minister Mackenzie King sit for a photo opportunity at the second Quebec Conference in September of 1944. *Photo Courtesy National Archives.*

At the outset of World War II in Europe, President Roosevelt told Americans, "When peace has been broken anywhere, the peace of all countries everywhere is in danger." It was this belief that led Roosevelt to insist upon supporting Great Britain during the Battle of Britain, and the same belief became the foundation of his close-working relationship with Winston Churchill and the other Allied leaders.

The close friendship and working relationship between Franklin Roosevelt and Winston Churchill brought their wives, Eleanor Roosevelt and Clementine Churchill, into contact. The two women were worlds apart. Mrs. Churchill's public role was very limited, and the prime minister held very traditional views about the proper public duties of women. Mrs. Roosevelt's involvement in matters of public policy, her speeches, her frequent travel, and her willingness to disagree with the president all struck Churchill as odd; conversely, Mrs. Roosevelt found Mrs. Churchill's reserve strange and the prime minister's views unenlightened, especially given British women's active participation in the war effort.

CHATEAU DE FRONTENAC, QUEBEC CITY—Eleanor Roosevelt and Clementine Churchill are pictured as part of a Canadian radio broadcast in September of 1944. *Photo U.S. Signal Corps, Courtesy National Archives.*

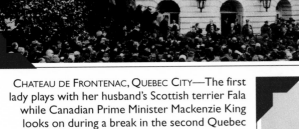

THE WHITE HOUSE, WASHINGTON, D.C.—President Franklin D. Roosevelt, after an unprecedented fourth election to the presidency, prepares to deliver his inaugural address from the portico of the White House, January 1944. *Photo International News, King Features.*

Let me assure you that my hand is the steadier for the work that is to be done, that I move more firmly into the task, knowing that you—millions and millions of you—are joined with me in the resolve to make this work endure....And to all Americans who dedicate themselves with us to the making of an abiding peace, I say: The only limit to our realization of tomorrow will be our doubts of today. Let us move forward with strong and active faith.
President Franklin D. Roosevelt
Warm Springs, Georgia
April 11, 1945

CHATEAU DE FRONTENAC, QUEBEC CITY—The first lady plays with her husband's Scottish terrier Fala while Canadian Prime Minister Mackenzie King looks on during a break in the second Quebec Conference, September 1944. *Photo U.S. Signal Corps, Courtesy National Archives.*

In a fireside chat on February 23, 1942, President Roosevelt asked the American people to take out an atlas and follow along as he described the World War II battlefields in the Pacific. With eighty percent of Americans tuned in, the president spoke of recent defeats in the Pacific and assured the people that the "government has unmistakable confidence in your ability to hear the worst without flinching or losing heart." Roosevelt spent days perfecting his speeches, carefully crafting the words that so many Americans relied upon for comfort and inspiration.

FORT OGLETHORPE, GEORGIA—President Roosevelt takes a break from a second war plant tour to visit the Third Women's Army Corps (WAC) Training Center. Standing at attention behind the president is Colonel Oveta Culp Hobby, director of the WAC, who later served as secretary of the Department of Health, Education, and Welfare under President Eisenhower. *Photo Courtesy National Archives.*

SELECTIVE SERVICE AND TRAINING

In 1939, the American Army ranked seventeenth in the world in total manpower and weapons. By law, it was limited to 375,000 men. In short, the armed forces of the United States were ill-prepared for war. This began to change in September of 1940, however, when Congress passed the Selective Service Act, which implemented the first peacetime military draft in American history. Opposition to the draft ran high, and some went so far as to call it an end to democracy in America; but the majority of Americans agreed with President Roosevelt that the building of our armed forces was essential in the face of the war that was moving ever closer to American shores. On October 29, 1940, with the president and a packed auditorium looking on, a blindfolded Secretary of War Henry Stimson drew the lottery numbers that would determine the order of induction for the American men age twenty-one to thirty-five who had registered with their local draft boards. In the months that followed, forty-six new training camps were built as the American armed forces swelled to nearly 1.5 million strong. When the time came for the United States to enter World War II, the armed forces, though still building and training, were prepared to fight.

Greetings:

Having submitted yourself to a local board composed of your neighbors for the purposes of determining your availability for training and service in the land or naval force of the United States, you are hereby notified that you have been selected for training and service therein. This local board will furnish transportation to an induction station. You will there be examined, and if accepted ... you will then be inducted into the land or naval forces.... Willful failure to report promptly to this local board at the hour on the day named ... is a violation of the Selective Service and Training Act of 1940, as amended, and subjects the violator to fine and imprisonment.

from an induction notice
mailed to draftees during World War II

NEW LONDON, CONNECTICUT—
Young students study at a submarine training school, August 1943. *Photo Courtesy National Archives.*

KINGSVILLE FIELD NAVAL AIR TRAINING COMMAND, CORPUS CHRISTI, TEXAS— Aviation cadets in the ready room await hops. *Photo Courtesy National Archives.*

The draft allowed for the buildup of manpower, but it took an enormous follow-up effort of training and instruction to turn civilians into soldiers. The camps to house and train the new recruits were put up quickly and often haphazardly. Senator Harry S Truman, head of a special committee investigating the defense program, reported, "If our plans for military campaigns are no more extensive and no better than [those for the camps], then we are in a deplorable situation." But despite the troubled and slow start, the drafted men and the volunteers who joined them became a powerful and efficient army. In the words of Sir Alan Brooke, the British chief of staff, the American soldiers "had a lot to learn.... but in the art of war ... when they got down to it, they were determined to make a success of it."

The Selective Service Act of 1940 provided that men would serve for twelve months before discharge. In the late summer of 1941, as the one-year anniversary of the Act drew near, Congress narrowly approved an eighteen-month extension to the term of service for draftees. A single vote allowed the expansion of the armed forces to continue and averted a decimation of forces that would have left the United States helpless to respond to the surprise attack on Pearl Harbor only months later.

CIVILIAN DEFENSE

The Office of Civil Defense was created by President Roosevelt in the spring of 1941. Its founding purpose was to encourage the citizens of the United States to become involved in building and maintaining the nation's defenses by volunteering in their home communities. The concept of civil defense covered a broad range of activities. One and a half million civilians volunteered as enemy plane spotters. They memorized the silhouettes of German and Japanese planes and filled their shifts watching the skies; enthusiasm seemed little dampened by the fact that not one of the volunteers ever spotted an enemy plane. Volunteers were also named air raid wardens, security guards, and fire fighters. Perhaps the most widely popular program was the Victory Garden. Encouraged to grow their own food so that farmers could concentrate on feeding the armed forces, Americans responded with more than 20 million garden plots that sprouted everywhere from city parking lots to jail yards to suburban lawns. Equally popular were war bonds. At rallies nationwide hosted by the country's most beloved celebrities, billions of dollars worth of bonds were sold. In a nation where nearly every family eventually saw a loved one go off to war, those at home showed their patriotism and support in their willingness to contribute in whatever way was asked.

War bonds funded the fight for freedom and also gave American citizens a solid way to contribute to the war effort. Nearly $50 billion worth of bonds were sold during wartime, a great majority thanks to the efforts of American celebrities— actors, actresses, singers, and others who used their names and notoriety to draw the crowds. Kate Smith was one prominent bond representative, as was actress Carole Lombard. Ms. Lombard, the young wife of Clark Gable, an actor turned Air Force gunner, lost her life in a plane accident after a war bond rally in Indianapolis during which she helped sell $2.5 million worth of bonds.

One of the many posters urging Americans to buy war bonds to pay for the material and weapons necessary to fight the war. *Photo Courtesy National Archives.*

A government poster urges Americans to accept some responsibility in wartime. *Photo Courtesy National Archives.*

Before December 7, 1941, World War II seemed distant and removed from my family in Woburn, Massachusetts, but this changed after Pearl Harbor was attacked by the Japanese and America entered the war; suddenly, the entire nation became focused and unified, and war was on everyone's mind. What I remember most about those years is the tremendous show of patriotism. People never complained too loudly about the sacrifices the war forced them to make. Milk, butter, eggs, gasoline, meat, and cigarettes were all rationed, and our red and blue cardboard tokens became our most valuable possessions. It was different, and sometimes difficult, but when the occasional complaint was heard, it was generally followed by the familiar retort "Don't you know there is a war on?"

I remember our Saturday morning family ritual during those years: my mother would drop me off at Kennedy's Butter and Egg Store downtown with my sisters, where we would wait in long lines with tokens firmly grasped in our small hands so that we could get our supplies for the week; Mother, meanwhile, was off to the butcher to get in line for our weekly meat allowance.

It also seemed that all of Hollywood and its celebrities were behind the fight for freedom. The movie stars were always staging huge rallies at which they sold war bonds—everyone who could was anxious to buy to help finance the nation's battles. Patriotic movies were the norm; they depicted American victories against tremendous odds. I remember people in the movie houses would stand up and cheer when the movie was over, for they wanted somehow to show their support for those involved in faraway battles. Even as a small child who could not truly understand the meaning of war, I felt the strong bond of patriotism that held us all together. In many ways, life during the war went on as usual. We went to school; we worked; we played; but the mood of the nation—the patriotism, the unity—touched us all. It is something I have never forgotten and something I have never felt again since those days.

Peter Skarmeas

SCRAP DRIVES AND RATIONING

In an April 1942 address to the nation, President Roosevelt told the millions of listeners gathered around their radios that although the war was being fought on faraway battlefields, there was "one front and one battle where everyone in the United States—every man, woman, and child—is in action....That front is right here at home, in our daily tasks." The president was speaking about a new program of rationing and resource conservation begun to support the war effort. The American people, eager to do what they could to support friends and family in the armed forces and speed the end of the war, accepted the president's plans with a solemn, if not always enthusiastic, sense of duty. The basic rationing system assigned points to each rationed item—meat, butter, sugar, coffee, canned and frozen foods—and issued each citizen a book of point stamps. The points could be used for any rationed item, but when the month's supply was gone, there were no more to be had. Some restrictions were deemed unacceptable; when the government called upon women to give up their girdles in the drive to collect and conserve rubber and suggested that women "grow their own muscular girdles, by exercise," the female population took objection. The government ultimately relented and classified girdles as an essential part of the American woman's wardrobe. Men willingly accepted the much smaller changes in their own dress—the "victory suit," which featured cuffless pants and narrow lapels, was designed to conserve cloth. While Americans learned to do without, they also learned the art of recycling. Tin cans, waste paper, aluminum, cooking grease, and more were collected in scrap drives, often in such great quantities that the supply outweighed the demand. On the home front, Americans proved skilled and eager combatants.

HOLLYWOOD, CALIFORNIA—Actress Rita Hayworth proudly displays her bumperless car, the metal bumpers having been donated as scrap metal. *Photo Courtesy National Archives.*

Wartime put heavy restrictions on one of America's favorite pastimes—driving. New cars stopped arriving in show rooms and were soon entirely unavailable. Gas was strictly rationed, as were tires, and new signs along the roadside proclaimed a "victory speed limit" of thirty-five miles per hour.

Nearly 200 million copies of Ration Book Number One rolled off the presses in March of 1942. Rationing began with sugar and coffee and later came to include a long list of grocery items, as well as such essentials as shoes and nylon stockings.

AN ELEMENTARY SCHOOL IN VIRGINIA—Grade-school children learn how to shop with point stamps. *Photo Courtesy National Archives.*

In April of 1945, I was a senior at Henry Clay High School in Lexington, Kentucky, a bobbysoxer about to turn eighteen. Our school was named for Lexington's most famous citizen. Orator, statesman, and three-time presidential candidate Henry Clay had dominated Kentucky politics during three decades of the nineteenth century.

Now, almost a hundred years after Clay's death, World War II, in its fourth year, was the context of our lives. We all knew boys in the service. Many meals at home were interrupted by phone calls bringing sad news, and my father, a Presbyterian minister, would often leave us to comfort a grieving family in the congregation.

Sacrifice was a word made real. While we chafed at its constraints sometimes, we were used to it by 1945. We spent our allowance on savings stamps; we did without field trips; we gave up class rings and our senior yearbook. Gasoline, tires, precious metals, paper—all went to the war effort. We also collected scrap metal, tons of it. Kettles, fences, garbage cans, old car parts, lawn mowers—people were asked to donate all metal items for defense, and donations were collected on specified days. A picture taken in front of Henry Clay High School during the war shows fifteen tons of the stuff piled on the lawn.

After school on April 12, a bunch of us piled in the back of the Lexington Victory Corps truck to take part in another scheduled scrap pickup. As it happened, our route took us into my neighborhood that afternoon. We didn't know then that this would be our last scrap metal drive.

We left school in a festive mood. News from Europe was encouraging. The sun was shining, forsythia was in bloom, tulips and daffodils filled every yard. But when we turned onto Second Street off North Broadway, a classmate hailed us, waving an extra edition of the Lexington Leader. The headline proclaimed the terrible news: "President Roosevelt Dead."

To hear that Mr. Roosevelt was dead subdued us as little else could have that afternoon. Our memories did not reach far back enough to know any other president, and we wondered what would happen to the war, to our country, to ourselves.

I'm sure we finished our rounds, but for me time stopped at the corner of Second and Broadway that afternoon. Today, fifty years later, I can still see that truck in the quiet street, my classmate on his bike, the awful headline, and all of us suddenly silent.

The war continued as the country mourned. Adults wept. My family mourned Mr. Roosevelt's death as we

would a death in the family. He had given us hope. He was gone.

The peaceful succession provided for in our Constitution gave us a new president, but we were uneasy with Harry Truman for a long time. Three weeks after Roosevelt died, the war in Europe ended. In August, America dropped two atomic bombs on Japan to end World War II, and our lives changed forever.

Marian Morris-Zepp

A government poster depicts the power of collected scrap metal. *Photo Courtesy National Archives.*

LEXINGTON, KENTUCKY— Piles of scrap metal in front of Henry Clay High School during World War II attest to the students' support for the war effort. *Photo Courtesy of J. Winston Coleman Photographic Collection, Transylvania University Library. Lexington, Kentucky.*

BLACK AMERICANS IN WORLD WAR II

Americans answered their country's call to service at the outset of World War II with great enthusiasm and patriotism; for a large segment of the population, however, that enthusiasm and patriotism was met by racism and discrimination. In the summer of 1940, fewer than 5,000 of the nearly one-half million men in the regular Army of the United States were black, and there was not a single black member of the U.S. Marine Corps or the Army Air Corps. Many with special skills who volunteered were simply turned away; those who signed up for service in the Navy were accepted readily but restricted to duty as messmen, responsible for cleaning and laundry. In June 1941, President Roosevelt issued an executive order forbidding discrimination on the basis of race in the armed forces. Throughout the war, countless black men and women served with honor and courage; but despite Roosevelt's order, the forces remained segregated. True acceptance and integration did not come until 1948, when President Harry Truman, perhaps in great part due to the record of black American skill and valor during World War II, issued Executive Order 9981, which eliminated segregation in the military.

One of the first heroes of World War II was a Navy black man, Dorie Miller. During the attack on Pearl Harbor, Miller, a messman, rescued his captain, then picked up a rifle and continued to fire on the Japanese planes, despite orders to abandon ship, until the ammunition was exhausted.

FORT BRAGG, NORTH CAROLINA—The 41st Engineers, an all-Black unit, participate in a color guard ceremony. *Photo U.S. Signal Corps, Courtesy National Archives.*

ABOARD THE USS *COWPENS*— Captain H.W. Taylor awards Fred Magee, Jr., St3/c a commendation of the secretary of the Navy for attempting to rescue, at great personal risk, a shipmate from drowning. *Photo U.S. Navy, Courtesy National Archives.*

SOMEWHERE IN ENGLAND— February 15, 1945, Major Charity Adams and Captain Abbie Campbell inspect the first contingent of black members of the Women's Army Corps (WAC) assigned to overseas service. The WAC gave the enlisted woman the best chance for overseas duty—the Navy, Marines, and Coast Guard limited women to service in the U.S. *Photo Courtesy National Archives.*

On March 7, 1942, five black pilots graduated from the Tuskegee Institute into the Army Air Corps. The Civilian Pilot Act of 1939 had laid the groundwork for the opening of this pilot training center in Tuskegee, Alabama. By 1942, one thousand Tuskegee Airmen had been trained for service. During the war, the Tuskegee Airmen distinguished themselves in Allied campaigns over North Africa, Italy, and Germany.

TUSKEGEE INSTITUTE, TUSKEGEE, ALABAMA—An instructor teaches Negro Air Corps cadets at Tuskegee the skills of sending and receiving Morse code. *Photo U.S. Signal Corps, Courtesy National Archives.*

NORFOLK, VIRGINIA—The Seabees, whose training center is at Camp Allen and Camp Bradford, practice landing tactics. *Photo Courtesy National Archives.*

AIR CORPS SCHOOL AT TUSKEGEE, ALABAMA—Howard A. Wooten, a December 1944 graduate and new member of the Tuskegee Airmen. *Photo Courtesy National Archives.*

Of the 2.5 million black Americans who served in World War II, more than 900,000 were in the Army. Three quarters of these soldiers served in the service branches, including the quartermaster, engineer, and transportation corps. One of the most celebrated transport divisions was the Red Ball Express, which delivered supplies to the troops on the front lines during the Allied advance on Germany. More than 150,000 blacks served in the Navy. The Marines had 2,000 black men among its ranks; the Coast Guard counted 5,000. Black women also found the services beginning to open up to them during World War II. Thousands served in the Army Nurse Corps, including three divisions which were sent overseas. Black women were also part of the newly begun Women's Army Corps (WAC) and Women Accepted for Volunteer Emergency Service (WAVES).

THIRTY SECONDS OVER TOKYO

When asked about the origins of the sixteen B-25 bombers that completed a successful surprise raid on Tokyo, Japan, on April 18, 1942, President Roosevelt's playful answer was, "They came from a secret base in Shangri-la." The bombers did little real damage, but their mission gave a boost to sagging American morale, dealt a blow to Japanese confidence, and may well have turned the tide of the war. The United States had struggled in the Pacific since the attack on Pearl Harbor, and Japan continued to boast of its invulnerability to attack; in "thirty seconds over Tokyo," all this changed. Led by Lieutenant Colonel James H. Doolittle, the hand-picked pilots flew normally land-based bombers off the decks of the carrier USS *Hornet*, taking off 800 miles from the Japanese coast. The Japanese detected the *Hornet* but believed it to be too far offshore to a be a threat since normal carrier planes had a range of only 300 miles; thus the American bombers reached Tokyo unscathed, dropped their barrage, and headed for an airfield inside China. When word of the raid reached the United States, Doolittle and his pilots were hailed as heroes, and Americans celebrated the first good news from the war in the Pacific. James Doolittle later received the Congressional Medal of Honor for his bravery.

The selection of Doolittle to lead this nearly suicidal mission was a natural one ... he was fearless, technically brilliant, a leader who not only could be counted upon to do a task himself if it were humanly possible, but could impart his spirit to others.

General Henry Arnold

ABOARD THE USS *HORNET*—Captain Marc A. Mitscher, right, skipper of the USS *Hornet*, chats with James Doolittle as some of the eighty flyers who took part in the Tokyo raid look on. *Photo U.S. Navy, Courtesy National Archives.*

Lieutenant Colonel James Doolittle was a forty-five-year-old veteran of World War I when he was chosen to plan and carry out the April 1942 raid on Tokyo. He chose his pilots carefully. "They were picked crews," he later remarked. "They were the crews that had the most experience with the airplane, ... they were absolutely topflight." One of the main problems involved in launching land-based planes from the decks of a carrier was runway length. If the bombers did not reach speeds necessary for takeoff before reaching the end of the deck, they would drop over the edge and be pierced by the front end of the ship. For a month in Florida, the pilots practiced the 750-feet takeoffs necessary for a carrier-based assault, but their takeoff from the Hornet was the first actual carrier launch for all sixteen men. When Lieutenant Colonel Doolittle, the first to take off, approached the end of the deck, a voice shouted that he would never make it; a split second later, Doolittle was in the air and on his way to Tokyo.

*B*ecause the USS Hornet *was spotted by a Japanese patrol boat, the raid on Tokyo was launched about ten hours sooner than planned and several hundred miles further from shore than intended. The result was that although the raid was successful, nearly all of the planes were forced to crashland in China; one went down in Japan, where three of its crew members were eventually executed. Despite this tragedy, seventy-one of the eighty pilots returned safely to the United States. After the Doolittle raid on Tokyo, the Japanese began to lose confidence in their invulnerability. In the coming months, they accelerated their plans for expansion in the Pacific and launched an unsuccessful attack on Midway Island.*

USS *HORNET*—One of Doolittle's pilots successfully takes off from the Navy carrier's flight deck. *Photo U.S. Navy, Courtesy National Archives.*

ON THE DECK OF THE USS *HORNET*—The long trip toward Tokyo begins with the liftoff of the first of the land-based planes from the flight deck of the carrier *Hornet. Photo U.S. Navy, Courtesy National Archives.*

ENGLAND'S SACRIFICES

In the late summer of 1940, the German Air Force, the Luftwaffe, began the intensive bombing of England that was meant to bring the nation to its knees in surrender to Adolph Hitler. The Battle of Britain began with the bombing of airfields and radar stations along the British coast; in September, the bombers zeroed in on London itself. In what is known as "the Blitz," German planes dropped their bombs on London day and night—and, when they could maintain that furious pace of attack no longer, by night alone—from September 1940 through June 1941. The Germans expected a quick capitulation, but the British, led by

Winston Churchill and the courageous pilots of the Royal Air Force (RAF), fought back valiantly and stood their ground. As the RAF used radar to track and shoot down the planes of the Luftwaffe, which outnumbered them by three to one, the citizens of London carried on through the chaos and destruction. They organized Home Guards to manage bomb shelters and other emergency services and Disposal Squads to daily defuse unexploded bombs. With American support in the form of ships and planes and weapons, the British withstood immeasurable damage and loss and ensured the survival and sovereignty of their nation.

LONDON, ENGLAND—Standing up gloriously out of the flames and smoke of surrounding buildings, St. Paul's Cathedral is pictured during the great fire raid of December 29, 1940. *Photo Courtesy National Archives.*

SMALL TOWN IN ENGLAND—British women share hot coffee with U.S. soldiers. *Photo Courtesy National Archives.*

Never in the field
of human conflict
was so much
owed by so many
to so few.

Winston Churchill, 1941
Speaking of the British RAF

LONDON— St. Paul's Cathedral stands unbowed in the middle of bomb-devastated London as a symbol of the city's and the nation's courage during the Battle of Britain, 1940-41.
Photo Courtesy National Archives.

As I listen to my mother-in-law, Brenda, tell stories of what it was like in her native England during World War II, I notice, by her expressions and the way she speaks, how much she enjoys these memories. She recalls how England and other European Allies were angered when Hitler marched into Poland; that's when her country joined in the war against Germany.

She was a young girl of nine years at the time, and wartime seen through the eyes of a child is different from what an adult sees. At her home in Dereham, in County Norfolk along the east coast of England, there were always soldiers staying with her family. She recalls an almost "party-like" atmosphere; the children loved the company and felt important with soldiers staying in their home. It was customary at this time for anyone with extra room to take in soldiers. Brenda's family took in many, and it was always hard to watch them leave, most likely to be never seen again. She recalls a special fondness for the "Yanks." They brought candy and gum—special treats that made a child's eyes sparkle during a time of strict rationing.

In Brenda's neighborhood, there was an orchard; it was in the orchard that the bomb shelter was built. Under a very large tree, a cave-like hole was dug by the neighborhood men; inside was cold, damp, and frightening. Often, despite the threat of bombs, the children would sneak out of the shelter in the middle of the night to pick fruit and play in the orchard. Other times, they could peer out of the opening and see the fires left by bombs burning in the distance.

To build the shelter, a local guard had been formed. The Home Guard was made up of elderly men and others who for one reason or another didn't qualify for military service.

Brenda's grandfather was a part of the Home Guard. A stubborn man, he helped build the shelter but never once heeded the call of the alarm—he spent his nights in his own home and defied the bombs that fell through the dark sky.

What seems terrible and frightening to us today was commonplace to British children like my mother-in-law. She remembers walking to the movies with her sister and ducking into the shrubs as an airplane flew overhead spraying machine-gun fire down the middle of the street. Their reactions were well-rehearsed, and the situation probably seemed to be a bit of a game to children unable to grasp the reality of war.

The bombing of Britain brought terror and suffering to countless people; nonetheless, my mother-in-law remembers it most of all as a time of great unity and courage. People came together, took care of one another, and shared all that they had. Brenda is quick to say that despite the war, she had a happy childhood.

Kathy Kelly

REGENT STREET, LONDON—August 10, 1945, shreds of paper fall from a window as news that Japan is negotiating for peace reaches London. *Photo Courtesy National Archives.*

PICCADILLY CIRCUS, LONDON—May 8, 1945, the city of London celebrates V-E Day. Hitler's fall and the occupation of Berlin brought great joy and relief to the people of England who, unlike Americans, had known the terror of war firsthand in their cities and towns. *Photo Courtesy National Archives.*

LONDON—An American soldier hugs an Englishwoman at Piccadilly Circus in London after learning of the surrender of Germany. *Photo Courtesy National Archives.*

THE RED CROSS

The Red Cross was over seventy-five years old when World War II began and had gained invaluable crisis experience during the First World War when it earned the nickname "The Greatest Mother" for its humanitarian efforts. After the attack on Pearl Harbor, tens of thousands of volunteers flooded the 4,000 U.S. chapters of the Red Cross looking for a way to serve their country; the Red Cross was prepared to put them to work. Volunteers rolled bandages—some 2.4 billion in all—collected blood, and brought books, magazines, music, and conversation to the wounded and lonely. Across America and overseas, Red Cross volunteers served out of a sense of common duty and brought a touch of humanity to the bleakest outposts of war.

NEW GUINEA—Red Cross field workers prepare Christmas gift boxes for shipment to soldiers in the Philippines in 1944. *Photo U.S. Signal Corps, Courtesy National Archives.*

MARKET SQUARE, NORTHAMPTON, ENGLAND—King George VI, at left, and Queen Mary of England visit a recently opened American Red Cross Club. The queen holds a bouquet of violets presented to her. *Photo U.S. Signal Corps, Courtesy National Archives.*

To Our Ill or Wounded Soldiers:

On this, another wartime Christmas, I would like to send you a personal message. We shall need your help when the war is won in the hard task of building a better and freer world. It is fitting, therefore, that at the Christmas time we who are older pledge that you who are younger shall be given the opportunity to fight for a better world in time of peace, as you have fought to save this lesser world in time of war. God bless you and keep you, for you belong to us and to the future of America.

Franklin D. Roosevelt
Commander in Chief
The White House
Christmas 1942

SOMEWHERE IN THE MIDDLE EAST—Servicemen on leave in the 9th U.S. Air Force enjoy a program by favorite American radio stars, played for them by a Red Cross volunteer. This record included Bob Hope, Jack Benny, Dinah Shore, and Harry James and was part of a weekly series produced by the Special Services of the U.S. Army. *Photo Courtesy National Archives.*

AID AND COMFORT

Men and women in every branch of service brought to the battlefields and hospitals of World War II gifts of caring and healing that saved many lives and brought moments of rest and peace to countless others.

36TH EVACUATION HOSPITAL ON LEYTE IN THE PHILIPPINES— First Lieutenant Phyllis Hocking adjusts glucose injection apparatus for a GI on December 24, 1944. The hospital was set up inside the Church of the Transfiguration, where services went on as usual. Behind Nurse Hocking, the congregation kneels in prayer. *Photo Courtesy National Archives.*

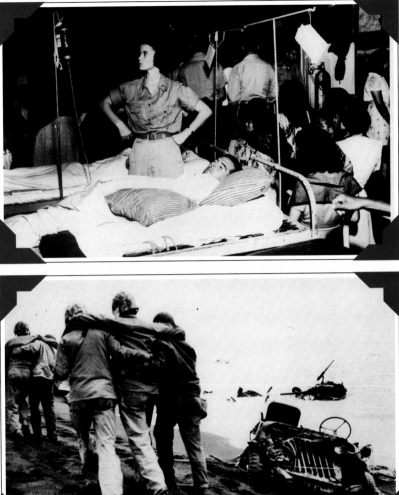

BATTLEFIELD SOMEWHERE IN FRANCE—Medics help an injured soldier. *Photo Courtesy National Archives.*

ON THE BATTLEFRONT—Navy corpsmen assist wounded marines in March 1945. *Photo Courtesy National Archives.*

I wasn't always a doctor. In World War II, I was a soldier. My basic training late in 1942 had been with the Military Police (MP) and in the next year I served with an MP company assigned to prisoner-of-war (POW) duty in the United States.

Successes in the African campaign which led to Rommel's defeat had brought German and Italian war prisoners to the States for confinement. Our first task was collecting trainloads of POWs who had been brought to New York and moving them across the United States by rail to POW camps at various locations. As the trains moved across the countryside, the immense landscape was a constant source of amazement for the POWs. Compared to countries such as Germany and Italy, the United States is huge. At breakfast, whole grapefruits were consumed in their entirety, skins and all. Those of us on breakfast detail, without knowledge of the language the prisoners spoke, could sense the impact of these experiences as we gazed at their faces. The situation was not a party, but neither was it a sorrow-laden affair.

Ultimately, my company was assigned to an Italian war prisoners camp in Como, Mississippi. We had lots of free time, and I remember organizing a circulating library for the staff with the United Service Organizations (USO) books that were available. At Thanksgiving, I even decorated the shelves with autumn leaves.

But I also recall coming down with pneumonia, which required hospitalization. I must have had a fever high enough to

have affected my mind, because I have no recollection of what transpired during my hospital stay. Shortly after returning to MP duty, my longstanding request for a transfer was granted; and the final year of the war, 1945, saw me as a combat infantry officer in the Philippine campaign.

Recently, while my wife and I were visiting a war buddy in Washington, D.C., I learned something I had never known about my hospitalization at the Como camp. My friend, the company clerk, had been a newspaper reporter during the war and had managed to keep daily records of his experiences. At the time of our visit, these were being transcribed. He asked my wife if she had heard the story about my being in the prisoner-of-war hospital with pneumonia and how the doctor who took care of me was an officer of the Italian Medical Corps. Unbelievable! Had the Army Manual of Regulations made any provision for such a contingency?

It was Army service that gave me the opportunity to attend medical school, and in 1951 I became a physician. Retired since 1986, I now know that circumstances over fifty years ago kept me from realizing the common thread of professional obligation that underlies the moral aspects of being a doctor—friend or foe of no concern. I also wonder now if I ever expressed my appreciation to that Italian exemplar of the healing arts.

Joseph M. Benforado, M.D.

THE BATTLE OF MIDWAY

After the shock of the American raid on Tokyo in April of 1942, the Japanese determined to reassert themselves and expand their territory in the Pacific. They set their sights on Midway Island, the westernmost American possession in the Pacific. From Midway, the Japanese would have the capability of launching further attacks on Hawaii, just over 1,000 miles away. But Admiral Yamamoto, who led the Japanese attack, did not count on either the skills of U.S. naval intelligence or the cunning of American Admiral Chester Nimitz, commander of the Pacific Fleet. Acting on detailed intercepted and decoded information about the impending attack on Midway, Admiral Nimitz quietly positioned his fleet—outnumbered four to one by the Japanese—a short distance from the island. Unmoved by a decoy attack to the north, Nimitz held his ground. At 9:30 a.m. on June 4, 1942, he ordered his men to strike. Torpedo bombers from the carriers *Enterprise*, *Hornet*, and *Yorktown*, followed by a squadron of dive bombers, launched a fierce attack on the invading Japanese fleet. The decisive battle was fought entirely by aircraft; Japanese and American carriers never drew within sight of each other. After four hard days of battle, the crippled Japanese fleet withdrew—awarding a monumental victory to the United States. No longer was Japanese naval power to be the ruling force in the Pacific.

IN THE SKIES AROUND MIDWAY ISLAND—Navy scout dive bombers fly over a burning submarine during the attack on the Japanese fleet off Midway Island, June 1942. *Photo U.S. Navy, Courtesy National Archives.*

Thanks in great part to the success of naval intelligence at breaking Japanese code, Admiral Nimitz was prepared for the Japanese assault at Midway, and his fleet scored a decisive victory. In addition to the 307 lives lost, American losses included one aircraft carrier and 150 aircraft. But the Japanese lost four carriers, over 300 aircraft, and 3,500 men—a terrible blow for Japanese naval leaders who believed themselves to be invincible in the Pacific.

ABOARD THE USS *SANTEE*—A typical ship's division on an escort carrier, one of a group of small carriers that provided close air support for amphibious landings. *Photo Courtesy Al Shively.*

THE BATTLE OF GUADALCANAL

The Battle of Guadalcanal would not end as quickly for the Pacific Fleet as the Battle of Midway had. On Guadalcanal, one of the Solomon Islands, the Japanese were building an airfield from which they could attack American ships headed to Australia. Realizing the strategic importance of the island, American leaders planned to take Guadalcanal. On August 7, 1942, ten thousand United States Marines went ashore at Guadalcanal Island; within a day they had taken the airfield. But when their Navy support was driven away, the Marines were stranded. Fighting continued on the island for six months before American victory was secured in February of 1943.

OFF THE COAST OF GUADALCANAL—Running a gauntlet of U.S. antiaircraft fire, four Japanese bombers come in low at Guadalcanal Island to attack U.S. transports. *Photo U.S. Navy, Courtesy National Archives.*

MARINE CAMP, GUADALCANAL—Marines keep up with news from home. The bulletin board posts official information and maps, as well as such reminders of home as professional baseball scores. The fighting on Guadalcanal Island was some of the fiercest of the war and was made worse for American Marines by the hot, rainy climate, the dense jungle, and the malaria which swept through their ranks. *Photo U.S. Navy, Courtesy National Archives.*

IN THE JUNGLE OF GUADALCANAL—The tents of the 43rd Division Hospital stand amid the jungle. *Photo U.S. Navy, Courtesy National Archives.*

Before World War II, most Americans had never heard of Guadalcanal Island, but for six months in 1942-43, it was home to thousands of young American men and on the minds of countless families back in the United States. Casualties during the Guadalcanal campaign were heavy as the land and sea battle raged. The Marines began the final push to gain control of the island in December 1942; by February 1943, the long, hard battle was won.

A Common Mission: The Allied Conferences

One of the great strengths of the Allies during World War II was their sense of common mission and cooperation. The fight against Hitler's Germany and the other Axis nations brought together a disparate group of nations and leaders, but they found grounds for compromise and in so doing found the strength to win the fight. American President Franklin Roosevelt and British Prime Minister Winston Churchill began the tradition of Allied cooperation in the summer of 1941 at the Atlantic Conference and followed up with two meetings in Quebec in 1943 and 1944. Roosevelt and Churchill invited Russia's

Josef Stalin to meet with them at conferences in Tehran and Yalta. By the time for the third and final Big Three conference in Potsdam in the summer of 1945, the deceased President Roosevelt had been replaced by President Harry Truman, and Churchill—in mid-conference—by newly elected Prime Minister Clement Attlee. Although the faces and locations changed, Allied resolve remained unchanged. While the Axis nations pursued their individual agendas, drawn together in a mutual pact of aggression, the Allied leaders put aside their differences to work together toward peace.

QUEBEC, CANADA—Roosevelt and Churchill meet at the railroad station prior to the second Quebec Conference. *Photo Courtesy National Archives.*

Franklin Delano Roosevelt and Winston Churchill first met face to face on August 9, 1941, aboard a ship off the coast of Newfoundland, Canada, at the Atlantic Conference. The purpose of their first meeting was to discuss American military aid to the British during the early years of World War II before America's official involvement. The two leaders would meet twice again on Canadian soil. At the first Quebec Conference in the summer of 1943, they laid the groundwork for Operation Overlord, the Allied invasion of France. At the second, in September of 1944, they discussed plans for the postwar treatment of Germany.

QUEBEC, CANADA—Gathered at the second Allied Conference at Quebec are, left to right, President Roosevelt, Canadian Prime Minister Mackenzie King, and Winston Churchill. Seated on the wall behind, from left to right, are Anthony Eden, British secretary of foreign affairs; Brendan Bracken, British minister of information; and Harry Hopkins, advisor to Roosevelt. *Photo Courtesy National Archives.*

*A*t Yalta, Josef Stalin began to show signs that he had wide-ranging plans of his own concerning the place of Russia in the post-war world. The other two leaders would be powerless to prevent Stalin's plans from becoming reality; President Roosevelt would be dead two months after Yalta, and Churchill would be voted out of office in five months.

*T*he biggest news at the final conference of Allied leaders in Potsdam actually originated thousands of miles away in New Mexico, where the first successful atomic explosion was carried out on July 15, 1945. President Truman was at Potsdam when he learned of the successful test. In the words of a War Department memo, the atomic bomb was "a revolutionary weapon destined to change war as we know it, or which even may be the instrumentality to end all wars."

*T*he Potsdam Conference began in July 1945 with a familiar face missing and finished in early August with only one of the original Big Three still in place. President Roosevelt had died the previous April; he was replaced at Potsdam by his successor, Harry S Truman. Winston Churchill arrived in Potsdam on schedule, but returned to England midway through the meetings for national elections. Churchill was voted out of office, and it was his successor, Clement Attlee, who finished out the meetings at Potsdam.

GENERAL DWIGHT DAVID EISENHOWER

Dwight D. Eisenhower was a lieutenant general when he was entrusted with the command of Operation Torch, the Allied invasion of Morocco and Algeria in the autumn of 1942. Eisenhower went on to lead the invasions of Sicily and the Italian mainland; and in the spring of 1944, as supreme commander of the Allied Expeditionary Forces, he planned and led the landing at Normandy, France, on D-Day. General Eisenhower was respected by his colleagues and loved by his men. He was restrained and tactful, a master of compromise and efficiency, and a brilliant and courageous leader. Among the first Americans to witness the liberated Nazi concentration camps in Germany, Eisenhower called upon the media of the United States and Great Britain to witness and report on Nazi atrocities so that the world would know the full truth about what had happened. After the war, Eisenhower's popularity remained strong; in 1952, he was elected to the first of two terms as president of the United States.

I hate war as only a soldier who has lived it can, only as one who has seen its brutality, its futility, its stupidity.

General Dwight D. Eisenhower

General Dwight Eisenhower began World War II as assistant chief of staff to General George C. Marshall in Washington, D.C. With Marshall and President Roosevelt, Eisenhower helped plan the nation's global strategy for war and laid the very first plans for an eventual cross-Channel invasion of France. From Washington, Eisenhower traveled to London as the commander of the European Theater of Operations and later as Allied supreme commander.

Soldiers, sailors, and airmen of the Allied Expeditionary Force: You are about to embark upon a great crusade toward which we have striven these many months. The eyes of the world are upon you. The hopes and prayers of liberty-loving people everywhere march with you. In company with our brave Allies and brothers-in-arms on other fronts, you will bring about the destruction of the German war machine, the elimination of Nazi tyranny over the oppressed peoples of Europe, and security for ourselves in a free world.

Your task will not be an easy one. Your enemy is well trained, well equipped, and battle hardened. He will fight savagely.

But this is the year 1944. Much has happened since the Nazi triumph of 1940-41. The United Nations have inflicted upon the Germans great defeat in open battle man to man. Our air offensive has seriously reduced their strength in the air and their capacity to wage war on the ground.

Our home fronts have given us an overwhelming superiority in weapons and munitions of war and placed at our disposal great reserves of trained fighting men.

The tide has turned. The free men of the world are marching together to victory.

I have full confidence in your courage, devotion to duty, and skill in battle. We will accept nothing less than full victory!

Good luck! And let us all beseech the blessing of Almighty God upon this great and noble undertaking.

General Dwight D. Eisenhower
D-Day Order of the Day
June 6, 1944

FRANCE—General Dwight Eisenhower greets Chief of Staff General George C. Marshall (center) and Justice James F. Byrnes (right), director of War Mobilization, upon their arrival aboard the first Air Transport Command to fly directly to France from the United States, October 6, 1944. *Photo U.S. Signal Corps, Courtesy National Archives.*

George Marshall chose Dwight Eisenhower as his assistant at the beginning of World War II due to Eisenhower's reputation as a brilliant tactician and a calm, intelligent leader. In an undertaking as great as the Allied war against Germany, Japan, and Italy, Marshall understood that administration and cooperation were to be as important as weapons and soldiers.

A 1948 poll of the American public found that General Dwight Eisenhower was the favorite of both the Republican and Democratic parties for the presidential nomination. Eisenhower, however, put off the potential "draft Ike" movement by accepting the presidency of Columbia University. By the time of the next presidential election, however, Eisenhower had declared himself a Republican and was ready to accept the nomination. A war hero who enjoyed the love and respect of a great cross section of Americans, Eisenhower won two terms in our nation's highest office.

Whatever America hopes to bring to pass in the world must first come to pass in the heart of America. The peace we seek, then, is nothing less than the practice and fulfillment of our whole faith among ourselves and in our dealings with others. This signifies more than the stilling of guns, easing the sorrow of war. More than escape from death, it is a way of life. More than a haven for the weary, it is a hope for the brave. This is the hope that beckons us onward ... this is the work that awaits us all to be done with bravery, with charity, and with prayer to Almighty God.

General Dwight D. Eisenhower

Eisenhower had the official jacket for the Army redesigned from a long coat to a waist-length jacket, which was more comfortable and practical for the fighting man. Dubbed the "Eisenhower jacket," the style was even popular in women's fashion for the period.

KANSAS CITY, MISSOURI—A soldier returning from war, General Eisenhower grins happily as he greets his mother, Mrs. Ida Eisenhower, while the general's brother Milton looks on, June 22, 1945. *Photo Bettman Newsphotos, Courtesy National Archives.*

D-DAY

On June 6, 1944, 170,000 men of the Allied Expeditionary Forces, supported by 5,000 ships and 11,000 aircraft, hit the beaches at Normandy, France. The attack, known as Operation Overlord, had been meticulously planned: aircraft would bomb German installations on the coast, paratroopers would land behind German lines, ships would open fire at a rate of 200 tons of shells per minute, and landing craft would deliver the men—from Europe, Africa, Asia, North America, and Australia—to the beaches.

The cross-Channel invasion was led by Supreme Commander General Dwight D. Eisenhower. On five beaches—Sword, Juno, Gold, Omaha, and Utah—the men fought valiantly and pushed inland. The Allies suffered heavily, particularly at Omaha Beach, where German defenses had escaped the bombing and met the landing force at near full strength. The landing, however, was the successful beginning of the drive through France and into Germany that would drive Hitler to surrender and end the war in Europe.

AN AIRFIELD IN ENGLAND—General Eisenhower gives the order of the day, "Full victory—nothing else," to paratroopers as they prepare to board their airplanes to participate in the first assault in the invasion of Europe at Normandy, June 6, 1944. *Photo Courtesy National Archives.*

Operation Overlord relied upon the courage and faith of hundreds of thousands of soldiers who risked their own lives for the greater cause of liberating Europe and the world from the tyranny of Hitler's Germany. The soldiers' courage was matched inside France by countless members of the resistance who laid some of the most important groundwork for the Allied arrival.

IN THE ENGLISH CHANNEL—Ships head toward Normandy during the Allied attack. Three and a half million men of the Allied forces gathered in England in the spring of 1944 in preparation for the June cross-Channel invasion. *Photo Courtesy National Archives.*

Although Operation Overlord would result in the final defeat of the Nazi war machine, the cost to the Allies was huge. The invasion was mounted with 6,939 naval vessels, 15,040 aircraft, and 156,000 troops. After two months, the casualties at Normandy numbered 16,434 dead, 76,535 wounded, and 19,704 missing. Within five months, the Allies had taken 637,544 prisoners and were on their way to the Rhine.

IN THE ENGLISH CHANNEL—Chaplain T. J. Fallon holds Roman Catholic service aboard the USS *Arkansas* off the coast of Normandy, France, before the Allied invasion. *Photo Courtesy National Archives.*

Give us faith in Thee; faith in our sons; faith in each other; faith in our united crusade.

General Dwight D. Eisenhower D-Day Prayer

ON BOARD THE USS *ARKANSAS*—Rear Admiral Alan G. Kirk visits the USS *Arkansas* to congratulate the men for their gallant performance in the invasion of France on D-Day. *Photo U.S. Navy, Courtesy National Archives.*

Along with the courage of his men, the months of careful study and planning, and the massive firepower of the Allied Expeditionary Forces, General Eisenhower relied upon the skills of his weathermen and a program of clever deception carried out by General George Patton to guarantee that the landing on the beaches at Normandy would be a success. The weathermen precisely forecast a break in the cloudy, stormy weather on the morning of June 6 that caught the Germans off guard and allowed Eisenhower to launch his assault. General Patton, acting on Eisenhower's instructions, created a decoy assault force in southeastern England to lead German intelligence to expect the attack at Pas de Calais, not Normandy.

THE ALLIED FORCES

After the Japanese attack on Pearl Harbor in December of 1941 and the subsequent Declaration of War by President Roosevelt, the United States found itself allied with twenty-five other nations from around the globe in opposition to the aggression of the Axis nations aligned behind Germany, Japan, and Italy. The Allies faced a long, deadly fight. In the six years of World War II, battles claimed the lives of almost 30 million people worldwide and wounded 30 million more. Over 46 million civilians lost their lives as well. Borders were redrawn, nations were renamed, great leaders were both made and brought down, and lives were forever altered. In the end, however, the Allied cause would prevail; for despite great differences in politics and culture, the United States and her allies found common ground and banded together in the fight for freedom and in the defense of peace.

In August of 1942, Winston Churchill appointed a new commander for the struggling British 8th Army in North Africa. Field Marshal Bernard L. Montgomery, a lean, tough, egotistical man, took the job without hesitation. "From now on," Montgomery declared, "the 8th Army will not yield a yard of ground to the enemy. Troops will fight and die where they stand." Montgomery's bold confidence gave a much needed boost to British morale, both on the battlefield and at home, and his leadership proved a valuable asset to the Allied cause.

*We come among you to repulse the cruel invaders.
…Help us where you are able. Viva la France éternelle!*

President Franklin Roosevelt, as U.S. Troops invaded French North Africa, 1942

MONTGOMERY HEADQUARTERS, ENGLAND—Allied generals, from left to right: Lieutenant General Sir Miles Dempsey, British 2nd Army; Major General Hodges, U.S. 1st Army; Field Marshal Sir Bernard Montgomery; Major General Simpson, U.S. 9th Army; and Lieutenant General Crerar, Canadian 1st Army. *Photo Courtesy National Archives.*

LONDON, ENGLAND—General de Gaulle, leader of the French Forces in Britain, inspects French troops during Bastille Day ceremonies in London. In Nazi-controlled France, this national Day of Free France on July 7, 1940, was observed in meditation only. *Photo Wide World Photos, Courtesy National Archives.*

During a radio broadcast from London to his countrymen and women in Nazi-occupied France, Charles de Gaulle declared, "The flame of resistance must not and will not be extinguished." De Gaulle, French under secretary of defense at the time of the German occupation, refused to accept Nazi domination of his homeland. Throughout the war, he remained devoted to his country's liberation and gave the French people a voice with Allied leaders. After Allied troops liberated Paris in August of 1944, de Gaulle rode triumphantly through the streets to cheers of "Vive de Gaulle!"

Under the command of General Douglas MacArthur, supreme Allied commander in the South Pacific region, the Australian 39th Infantry Battalion heroically and successfully defended the Kokoda Trail, which ran across the island of New Guinea, in 1942. The Japanese hoped to control the Kokoda Trail in order to gain access to Port Moresby on New Guinea's southern coast. From Port Moresby, the Japanese would be able to launch an attack on the Australian continent.

OFF THE COAST OF BORNEO—Australian troops pour ashore from an American-manned LST (Landing Ship, Tank) at Borneo, another of the contested islands off the Australian coast. *Photo U.S. Navy, Courtesy National Archives.*

The Potsdam conference, held near the war-ravaged German city of Berlin, came to an end only days before the American bombing of the Japanese cities of Hiroshima and Nagasaki, in August 1945, brought an end to the war. Weeks later, the leaders who met at Potsdam authorized their representatives to sign a peace agreement aboard the USS Missouri in Tokyo Bay, Japan. Generals and admirals of the United States, Great Britain, China, Russia, the Netherlands, New Zealand, Canada, France, and Australia signed the historic agreement for the Allies.

POTSDAM, GERMANY—A regiment of Scottish Highlanders pass in review before Prime Minister Winston Churchill during a parade of Allied troops at the Potsdam Conference in 1945. *Photo Courtesy National Archives.*

THE JOURNALISTS AND PHOTOGRAPHERS OF THE WAR

More than 700 correspondents covered the progress of World War II for American newspapers, magazines, and radio; the Allied landing at Normandy alone was reported by nearly 500 American journalists. On radio, men like Edward R. Murrow, who covered the bombing of London and flew as an observer in combat missions over Germany, became the voice of the war for American families. Robert Capa, Edward Steichen, and their fellow photographers created a visual record of war while cartoonists like Bill Mauldin, who gave us the GIs Willie and Joe, and George Baker, who created the everyman infantryman named Sad Sack, gave Americans in the service and at home a glimpse of GI life that was real and touching and funny all at once. In daily newspapers and weekly magazines, writers like the beloved Ernie Pyle made the names *Guadalcanal* and *Iwo Jima* a part of the American vocabulary and honored the daily struggles of the men and women in uniform. To Americans carrying on with their daily lives thousands of miles from the battlefields, Americans anxious for any information, these brave, dedicated journalists were their eyes and ears on the war.

ON A U.S. NAVY AIRCRAFT CARRIER—Edward J. Steichen perches atop an island platform for a better view of life aboard an aircraft carrier. *Photo U.S. Navy, Courtesy National Archives.*

You begin to feel that you can't go on forever without being hurt. I feel that I have used up all my chances. And I hate it. I don't want to be killed.

Ernie Pyle, 1945

Edward J. Steichen, already an award-winning photographer at the onset of the war and beyond the draft age, nevertheless joined the U.S. Navy and assembled a top-notch crew to photograph the war. Although in non-combat slots, the photographers and journalists, whether working for the military or commercial concerns, were constantly in danger. Many of them, like Ernie Pyle, were killed on the field of combat. Steichen, like countless other photographers and journalists, many of whom will forever remain anonymous, chronicled the war in all its aspects. Their work now stands as a record of the great sacrifices and struggles of World War II.

ABOARD THE USS *ENTERPRISE*—The third Japanese bomb hits the flight deck of the *Enterprise* on August 24, 1942. The photographer lost his life while taking this picture. *Photo Courtesy National Archives.*

*E*rnie Pyle was a middle-aged, gray-haired journalist who wrote about the experiences of the common soldier on the front lines of World War II. Pyle called the American GIs the "mud-rain-frost-and-wind boys"; to these men Ernie Pyle was a hero and a friend. Pyle wrote about war from the inside. He lived and traveled with the troops and celebrated the heroism of every anonymous soldier and sailor who put on a uniform.

ABOARD A U.S. NAVY AIRCRAFT CARRIER—Pyle mounts a breeches buoy for the ride across the water between an aircraft carrier and a destroyer during a survey of Navy life in the Pacific, March 27, 1945. *Photo U.S. Navy, Courtesy National Archives.*

Captain Burgess Meredith of the U.S. Army Air Force, an American stage and screen star, looks through the pages of *Here Is Your War* as author Ernie Pyle looks on. Meredith, on inactive duty, starred in the motion picture based on Pyle's book as well as films based on the writing of other American war correspondents. Like Pyle's writings, the movie celebrated the American soldier and the part he played in the war. *Photo Courtesy National Archives.*

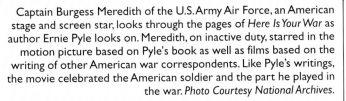

*T*he men of the 77th U.S. Army Infantry erected a memorial to journalist Ernie Pyle, who was with them on the Japanese island of Ie Shima when he was killed by machine gun fire in April of 1945. Of his firsthand experience of war, Pyle wrote, "I believe I have a new patience with humanity that I have never had before.... I don't see how any survivor of war can ever be cruel to anything ever again."

IE SHIMA—Memorial erected in the memory of Ernie Pyle by the men of the 77th U.S. Army Infantry Division. *Photo U.S. Army, Courtesy National Archives.*

ENTERTAINING THE TROOPS

On makeshift stages set up on truck beds or in jungle clearings, enduring poor lighting, terrible acoustics, and unpredictable weather, thousands of American performers—actors, singers, dancers, comedians, and anyone else who could put on a show—traveled the globe to bring a few moments of laughter and enjoyment to the men and women who were fighting on the front lines during World War II. The United Service Organizations (USO), with more than 3,000 clubs in the United States and countless traveling shows that made the rounds from the Pacific to Europe to China to Alaska's Aleutian Islands, brought such stars as Laurel and Hardy, Bing Crosby, Frank Sinatra, Fred Astaire, Ginger Rogers, Marlene Dietrich, Rita Hayworth, Errol Flynn, and Spencer Tracy to the troops. Perhaps the most devoted performers were Bob Hope, who made USO shows the trademark of his career, and Ann Sheridan, who logged 60,000 miles on a performance tour through China, Burma, and India and was so loved by the men of the armed forces that she received letters from wives who feared Ms. Sheridan had stolen their husbands' devotion.

Nearly 400 USO performers lost their lives while traveling to perform for the men and women of the armed services. One of the first and the most popular USO shows was put on by Laurel and Hardy. The comedy team fell out of favor with organizers, however, when they made a movie parodying the Office of Civilian Defense.

AUGSBERG, GERMANY—Carolyn Wall and Raymond Massey, appearing in the USO show "Our Town," serve dinner to the men of the 7th Army in July 1945. *Photo U.S. Signal Corps, Courtesy National Archives.*

ABOARD THE USS *ARKANSAS*—Crew members line topside to watch a USO show in North Africa. *Photo U.S. Navy, Courtesy National Archives.*

WAIKIKI BEACH, OAHU, HAWAII—Above, Bob Hope entertains on stage at the Naval Recreation Center. At left, Hope performs with Frances Langford at the naval hospital. *Photo U.S. Navy, Courtesy National Archives.*

IN A FIELD IN NORTHERN FRANCE—Bing Crosby sings to soldiers during a show sponsored by Special Services. Crosby was joined in this show by another popular American singer, Dinah Shore. *Photo Courtesy National Archives.*

SASEBO, JAPAN—Danny Kaye entertains occupation troops of the 5th Marine Division. *Photo U.S. Navy, Courtesy National Archives.*

NEAR MARSEILLE, FRANCE—GIs watch the Copacabana All Girl revue at the Glenn Miller Theater, August 1945. *Photo Courtesy National Archives.*

No one group did more to intensify and sustain the spirit of patriotism in the U.S. during World War II than the entertainment industry. The biggest stars in Hollywood made themselves available for USO tours. Top bands, singers, comedians, and actors visited hospitals and military bases at home and overseas to raise the morale of the GIs and let them know that they were not forgotten. New York City's famous Stage-Door Canteen was an oasis for lonely servicemen, far away from home and anxious about their futures. Stage and screen stars volunteered to spend time with the young GIs. The celebrities talked, danced, listened, served coffee, and lifted the spirits of the brave, young Americans who were on their way to war.

Hollywood studios worked overtime filming movies about the war; from the most heartbreaking stories of heroism and sacrifice, like The Fighting Sullivans, a true story about five brothers who enlisted in the Navy after Pearl Harbor and lost their lives aboard the same ship, to lighthearted comedies like Abbott and Costello's Buck Privates. Movies about the toll of the war on the people at home—such as Mrs. Miniver and The Best Years of Our Lives—helped fuel the fire of patriotism burning in all of us.

Whether movie stars were entertaining the troops, like Bob Hope, or selling bonds, or actually putting their careers on hold to serve in the armed forces, like Clark Gable, Jimmy Stewart, Henry Fonda, Tyrone Power, and many others, these men and women did the best they could with the talents they had to support their country. They were a true inspiration, and their entertainment was a distraction and a comfort.

Mary Theodore

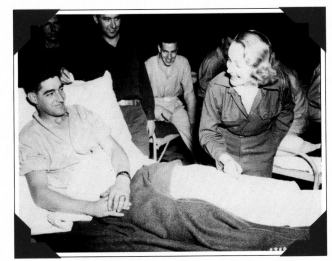

BELGIUM—Marlene Dietrich, while on a hospital tour, autographs a cast for an American soldier in November 1944. *Photo Courtesy National Archives.*

GMUND, GERMANY—USO show with Ingrid Bergman and Jack Benny, July 1945. *Photo U.S. Signal Corps, Courtesy National Archives.*

HEROES IN THE AIR: THE FLYING TIGERS

Throughout World War II, while the attention of most Americans was focused on battles in Europe and the Pacific, there was a third theater of war—the China-Burma-India theater—where American forces were positioning themselves for an air attack on the Japanese islands. Under General Joseph Stilwell, who led ground forces in fighting along the Burma Road, and General Claire Chennault, who commanded the Allied Air Offensive over China, American troops in China engaged in some of the roughest fighting of the war. But none of this would have been possible if not for a group of pilots known as the Flying Tigers, who, before the United States officially entered the war,

"flew the hump" over the Himalayas to bring supplies to China. The Flying Tigers were assembled by General Chennault, who was in China as an advisor to Chiang Kai-shek, the Chinese leader. In eight months in 1941, the Flying Tigers flew the skies over China with unmatched success, shooting down 300 Japanese aircraft and maintaining a life-sustaining flow of supplies to the Chinese people. The Flying Tigers helped keep China in the war and out of Japanese hands. When the United States officially entered World War II, the Flying Tigers were merged into the Army Air Force, but their contribution to the Allied cause would not soon be forgotten.

SOMEWHERE IN CHINA—A Chinese soldier guards a line of American P-40 fighter planes that are painted with the shark-face emblem of the Flying Tigers in 1942. *Photo Office of War Information, Courtesy National Archives.*

General Claire Chennault assembled his legendary Flying Tigers from a group of 100 recently retired U.S. military pilots and 200 crew members. Although at the time he was said to be operating under the authority of the Chinese government, it has since been revealed that Chennault had full American approval and support for his efforts to aid China in her fight against Japan. Chennault, called "Old Leather Face" and regarded as a hero by the Chinese people, was a member of the U.S. Army Air Service in World War I in the earliest days of military aviation.

ON A MAKESHIFT BASEBALL FIELD—Major General Gilbert Cheves (left) and Major General Claire Chennault observe a typically American custom by opening a softball game in China. Chennault pitched for the Flying Tigers, and Cheves held down first base for the opposition. *Photo Courtesy National Archives.*

FLYING TIGERS COMMAND POST—Major General Claire Chennault directs operations at his command post during a Japanese air raid. *Photo U.S. Navy, Courtesy National Archives.*

THE AIR WAR

During World War II, advances in aviation technology made the air a vital battleground. In Europe, the Pacific, and China, American aircraft fought to rule the skies. Probably no other World War II aircraft was as well known as the American B-17, nicknamed the "Flying Fortress." In 1943, the Allies began an unprecedented bombing campaign over Germany. By night, British bombers flew scatter bombing raids; by day, the pilots of the U. S. 8th Air Force flew B-17s in strategic raids on military and industrial targets. The B-17s lived up to their nickname during these raids; stories abound of the massive damage they received while still making it home. Still they were not invulnerable; during raids on the Schweinfurt ball bearing works and the Messerschmitt factory in Regensburg, Germany, in 1943, sixty B-17s and their crews were lost. After these losses, B-17s were equipped with machine guns for self-defense, thirteen on each plane by war's end. Along with the planes of the RAF, American B-17s helped weaken both enemy defenses and the morale of the German people. By the end of 1944, Berlin had suffered twenty-four major air raids and much of Germany was without water, lights, and heat. The leading role in the air war, however, went not to the Flying Fortress, but to a plane nicknamed the "Liberator"—the B-24. More B-24s were produced than any other American combat plane. Used mostly in the Pacific, B-24s are best remembered for their bombing raids on the oil fields at Ploesti, Poland, in August 1943. One hundred and seventy-eight B-24s flew 1,500 miles from Libya across the Mediterranean and the German-occupied Balkans into Poland. The planes met resistance by German fighters, but obliterated the oil fields. American losses were high, however; only thirty-three of the planes returned to fly again. The B-24s and the B-17s, along with the rest of the aircraft, pilots, and crew members of the American Army Air Corps, were indispensible to the Allied cause. In a war that reached nearly every corner of the globe, mastery of the air was a prerequisite to victory.

OVER PARIS, FRANCE—A photograph from a B-17 captures the impact of its bombing attack on a ball-bearing plant in December 1943. *Photo Courtesy National Archives.*

OVER MARIENBURG, POLAND—The first big raid by the 8th Air Force is carried out over a plant in Poland in 1943. The Germans were in full force, and the Allieds lost at least eighty planes and 800 men. *Photo Courtesy National Archives.*

The Allied bombers so ruled the skies of Europe that on D-Day, General Eisenhower reassured his troops with this quip: "If you see fighting aircraft over you, they will be ours."

SOMEWHERE OVER EUROPE—Two B-17 bombers drop their loads over Europe. *Photo Courtesy National Archives.*

THE BATTLE OF THE BULGE

In December of 1944, Allied forces in France were engaged in what General Eisenhower called "the dirtiest kind of infantry slugging." General Patton's 3rd Army had fought its way through the Siegfried Line, the concrete fortification built to stop the Allied advance through France and into Germany, and, after a week of street fighting, had captured the French city of Metz. At the same time, the Allied armies had gathered along the French eastern border ready to plunge into Germany. Allied plans for immediate advance were foiled, however, by a furious Nazi counteroffensive. The Germans reversed their retreat and pushed back against the Allied forces, creating the bulge in the Allied line that would give the ensuing battle its name: the Battle of the Bulge. There followed one of the fiercest land battles of the war. The Allies found themselves trapped in the Ardennes Forest at Bastogne, Belgium. On December 17, the 18,000 men of the 101st Airborne Division, then 100 miles behind the lines, were ordered to Bastogne as reinforcements. The American situation, nonetheless, appeared hopeless. The thick cloud cover prevented both bombing and the delivery of supplies; the men were stranded and starving. On December 22, recognizing the Americans' desperation, the Germans presented a formal demand for surrender to General McAuliffe of the 101st Airborne. McAuliffe replied with the simplest of refusals: "Nuts!" The next day, the weather cleared and planes began dropping supplies and bombs. By December 26, 1944, Patton's 3rd Army had arrived, and Bastogne was saved. The Germans never again launched an effective counteroffensive.

ON THE WESTERN BORDER OF GERMANY—An aerial view shows a road passing through the Siegfried Line, which the Germans believed to be impassable. *Photo U.S. Signal Corps, Courtesy National Archives.*

The Battle of the Bulge cost Americans 80,987 casualties, including 19,000 killed and 15,000 captured. German losses included 120,000 men and 1,600 planes.

THROUGH THE SIEGFRIED LINE—Soldiers of an Allied Engineer Battalion guard the bridge through the Siegfried Line's "Dragon Teeth," which proved to be only a small deterrent to American forces. *Photo U.S. Signal Corps, Courtesy National Archives.*

OUTSIDE OF LA ROCHE, BELGIUM—Chow is served to American infantrymen in January 1945. *Photo Courtesy National Archives.*

NEAR CARENTAN, FRANCE— American howitzers shell retreating German forces. *Photo U.S. Signal Corps, Courtesy National Archives.*

CROSSING THE RHINE

By the end of January 1945, General Eisenhower was ready to lead his Allied troops across the Rhine River into Germany. The Rhine was not only a formidable moat on Germany's western border—a half-mile wide in some points—but in the minds of the Allied men, the river had taken on great symbolic value. To cross the Rhine would be to take a giant step toward victory. As the German army retreated, they blew up the bridges over the Rhine, hoping to slow the Allied advance. But on March 7, after securing the German city of Cologne, the American 1st Army discovered the only intact bridge across the Rhine, thirty miles south of Cologne in a little town called Remagen. A volunteer from the retreating army had attempted to trigger an explosion, but the demolition wires had been severed; the resulting partial explosion made the bridge shudder, but did not bring it down. Seizing this unexpected opportunity, the American troops charged across the bridge. When General Eisenhower learned of the crossing, he described it as "one of the happiest moments of the war." The crossing at Remagen was a symbolic victory; the main Allied assault into Germany lay several days ahead. As Allied forces massed along the Rhine in careful preparation for the group crossing and the assault on the waiting German defenses, however, American General George Patton found it impossible to wait. Patton's 3rd Army came upon a riverside cove, piled six battalions into boats, and paddled across the Rhine. They found only one platoon of German soldiers guarding the opposite bank. The next morning, Patton telephoned General Omar Bradley with the news of his crossing and warned, "Don't tell anyone I'm across." Later in the day, however, Patton could contain his pride no longer; again he phoned Bradley: "Brad, for God's sake, tell the world! I want the world to know that the 3rd Army made it . . . across." Days later, the gathered Allied forces followed the American 1st and 3rd Armies across the Rhine and into Germany—the days of Hitler's Third Reich were numbered.

On December 24, 1944, German aircraft unleashed a furious bombing assault on the town of Bastogne, Belgium. Inside Bastogne's chapel, the wounded lay on the stone floors wrapped in colored Army parachutes for warmth. As the choir sang "Silent Night, Holy Night," the wounded men joined in; for all gathered, it was a Christmas Eve to remember.

On April 6, 1944, with German defenses collapsing under the heavy assault of the American XVIII Airborne Corps during the Ruhr offensive, American General Matthew B. Ridgway sent a gracious letter to the German commander: "Neither history nor the military profession records any nobler character, any more brilliant master of warfare, any more dutiful subordinate of the state, than the American General Robert E. Lee. Eighty years ago this month, his loyal command reduced in numbers, stripped of its means of effective fighting and completely surrounded by overwhelming forces, he chose an honorable capitulation. "The same choice is yours now. In the light of a soldier's honor, for the reputation of the German officer corps, for the sake of your nation's future, lay down your arms at once." Because Hitler forbade surrender, German Field Marshal Model disbanded his command and ended his life with a single shot. The battle for the Ruhr ended, and 317,000 German troops surrendered.

NEAR RENTWERTSHAUSEN, GERMANY—A mammoth 274-millimeter railroad gun captured in the U.S. 7th Army advance holds twenty-two men lined up on the barrel, April 10, 1945. *Photo U.S. Army, Courtesy National Archives.*

SOMEWHERE IN EUROPE—Commanding General Matthew B. Ridgway, left, of the XVIII Airborne Corps shakes the hand of Field Marshal Bernard Montgomery. *Photo Courtesy National Archives.*

A Few of the Many Outstanding Military Leaders

In the trust of America's military leaders was placed not only the fate of the nation, but the individual lives of each and every soldier and sailor who put on a uniform. The brave and accomplished American admirals and generals of World War II plotted the strategies, planned the battles, rallied the troops, and helped lead the United States and the Allies to victory.

SOMEWHERE BETWEEN NORTH AFRICA AND SICILY—Lieutenant General Omar N. Bradley and Captain Timothy Wellings stand on the navigation bridge of the USS *Ancon* in July 1943. General Bradley, nicknamed the "soldier's soldier," was a modest, thoughtful, conscientious man, a careful planner who took charge of American troops as they pushed inward from the beaches of Normandy in the summer of 1944. A West Point classmate of Dwight Eisenhower, Bradley rose from the command of a single division to command of the entire U.S. 12th Army. On V-E Day, Bradley was a four star general; his fifth star was awarded after the war. Far from the stereotype of the cold, hard military man, Bradley was always sensitive to the emotional burden of war. "War," he once remarked, "is as much a conflict of passion as it is of force.... Far from being a handicap to command, compassion is the measure of it." *Photo U.S. Navy, Courtesy National Archives.*

General George C. Marshall (on the left) was chief of staff during World War II and one of Franklin Roosevelt's inner circle of advisors. A quiet, patient, thoughtful man, Marshall made his greatest impact on world history after the war when his Marshall Plan dictated American approach to the economic recovery of war-ravaged nations. In a simple sentence delivered as part of an address to the graduating class of Harvard University in 1947, Marshall declared that the United States "should do whatever it is able to do to assist in the return of normal economic health in the world, without which there can be no political stability and no assured peace." The Marshall Plan earned Marshall the Nobel Peace Prize in 1953 and has shaped American foreign policy for more than four decades. General Henry "Hap" Arnold (right) headed the Air Corps in the days when it was still a part of the Army. He was an innovative and determined man. It was Arnold who pushed for the development of the B-29, one of the most important planes in World War II, with his insistence that the Air Corps needed a plane that could fly longer distances and carry greater loads than any other aircraft in the world. Arnold also devised the plan for James Doolittle's raid on Tokyo in April of 1942, which proved a decisive and portentous victory for the United States in the Pacific. *Photo U.S. Signal Corps, Courtesy National Archives.*

PEARL HARBOR, HAWAII—Admiral Chester W. Nimitz, commander in chief of the United States Pacific Fleet, presents awards aboard the USS *Enterprise* in October 1942. A bold and confident leader, it was Nimitz who defeated the Japanese at Midway Island, a victory that may well have turned the tide of the war in the Pacific in America's favor. Nimitz was also a key man in the final push toward the Japanese mainland in 1945. *Photo Courtesy National Archives.*

WASHINGTON, D.C.—General Jonathan Wainwright is presented the Congressional Medal of Honor by President Truman in September 1945, following the liberation of the Japanese prison camp where Wainwright had been held. Lieutenant General Wainwright took charge of the weakened American forces in the Philippines when General Douglas MacArthur was ordered to leave the islands in 1942. As MacArthur vowed, "I will return," Wainwright mounted a heroic and inspiring defense of the Bataan Peninsula against larger and stronger Japanese forces. Wainwright eventually surrendered Bataan and retreated with part of his men to the island of Corregidor; the remainder were taken prisoner and marched seventy miles to prison camps. In what became known as the Bataan Death March, nearly half of these men died of malnutrition and starvation. Wainwright, meanwhile, held out in the tunnels of Corregidor's fort for as long as he could before surrendering along with 13,000 of his men. Before turning himself over to the Japanese, Wainwright sent a telegram to President Roosevelt: "With broken heart and head bowed in sadness but not in shame, I go to meet the Japanese commander." Wainwright was eventually released and stood behind MacArthur as the official surrender papers were signed aboard the USS *Missouri* in August 1945. *Photo U.S. Signal Corps, Courtesy National Archives.*

SOMEWHERE IN FRANCE—Brigadier General Benjamin O. Davis watches a Signal Corps crew in 1944. The first black general in the U.S. armed forces, Davis was the father of one of the first five graduates of the Tuskegee Institute pilot training program for black Americans. *Photo Courtesy National Archives.*

QUEBEC, CANADA—The U.S. Combined Chiefs of Staff assemble at the Quebec Conference of 1943. From left to right: General George C. Marshall, U.S. Army; General H. H. Arnold, U.S. Army Air Forces; General J. R. Dean, secretary to the Chiefs of Staffs; Admiral Ernest King, U.S. Navy; Admiral William Leahy, U.S. Navy. *Photo U.S. Signal Corps, Courtesy National Archives.*

MAYMYO, BURMA—General Joseph W. (Vinegar Joe) Stilwell poses with Generalissimo and Madame Chiang Kai-shek on April 19, 1942, the day following Doolittle's attack on Tokyo. A West Point graduate and World War I veteran, Stilwell saw more front-line combat than any other American four-star general in World War II. As commander of all American forces in the China-Burma-India theater, he directed the two-year construction of the Burma Road that ended the blockade of China. *Photo Courtesy National Archives.*

GENERAL GEORGE S. PATTON

Hot-headed and profane, spirited and never predictable, General George S. Patton, Jr., was one of the most colorful, memorable, and successful leaders of World War II. He led the American forces in North Africa and during the invasion of Sicily, and he organized the decoy invasion force that helped distract the Germans' attention from the Allied landing forces at Normandy, France, on D-Day. Patton then took charge of the U.S. 3rd Army and met up with the Allied landing forces as they broke through into the French interior. Leading his troops at record speed across the French countryside, Patton led the Allied defense at the Battle of the Bulge before his troops made their final push into Germany. A military man through and through, General Patton once declared that "compared to war, all other forms of human endeavor shrink to insignificance."

God of our fathers, who by land and sea has ever led us to victory, please continue Your inspiring guidance in this the greatest of our conflicts.
Strengthen my soul so that the weakening instinct of self-preservation, which besets all in battle, shall not blind me in my duty to my responsibility to my fellow soldiers.
Grant to our armed forces that disciplined valor and mutual confidence which ensures success in war.
Let me not mourn for the men who have died fighting, but rather let me be glad that such heroes have lived.
If it be my lot to die, let me do so with courage and honor in a manner which will bring the greatest harm to the enemy, and, please, O Lord, protect and guard those I shall leave behind.
Grant us the victory, Lord.

General George S. Patton
"The Soldier's Prayer"
Knutsford, England
January 1, 1944

RED RIVER, LOUISIANA—General George S. Patton, Jr., commander of the 2nd Armored Division at Fort Benning, Georgia, stands on the shore overlooking a bridge being built by the 17th and 87th Engineers Corps, September 8, 1941. *Photo U.S. Signal Corps, Courtesy National Archives.*

EUROPEAN THEATER—General Patton prepares to go aloft to inspect the forces of the United States 3rd Army, August 1944. Patton's leadership was instrumental in the Allied advance into Germany. *Photo U.S. Signal Corps, Courtesy National Archives.*

Let me not mourn for the men who have died fighting, but rather let me be glad such heroes have lived!

General George S. Patton

After the liberation of Paris in August of 1944, a triumphant General George Patton cabled in his trademark manner to General Eisenhower:"Dear Ike, Today I spat in the Seine."

Toward the end of World War II, General George Patton wrote to his wife, "Peace is going to be hell on me." The military gave Patton his sense of identity and purpose. He was not to face life long after World War II was ended, however. Patton died on December 21, 1945, twelve days after breaking his neck in an automobile accident in Germany. While the world mourned his passing, Patton was buried in the huge American military cemetery at Hamm in Luxembourg, where he joined 6,000 other heroes of the 3rd Army. The inscription on the plain white cross reads simply:
GEO. S. PATTON JR.
GENERAL. 02605. 3D ARMY

ST. MARTIN, AUSTRIA—General Patton rides a stallion confiscated by Adolph Hitler and intended as a personal gift to Emperor Hirohito of Japan. American forces under Patton freed the horse and returned it to its rightful home. For Patton, his role in the eventual advance into Germany was a satisfying redemption after a controversial incident in Sicily led General Eisenhower to remove him from any central role in the landings at Normandy during Operation Overlord. *Photo U.S. Signal Corps, Courtesy National Archives.*

GENERAL PATTON'S QUARTERS—Patton's pet bull terrier Willie is shown with Patton's trunks after the general's death. *Photo Courtesy National Archives.*

MILITARY LIFE

Fifteen million American draftees and volunteers served in the various branches of the armed forces between 1940 and 1945. For many, World War II was part of a lifelong military career; for others, it was a first experience of the world outside their hometown. For all, however, it was at times frightening, lonely, painful, frustrating, exciting, educational, and just plain dull. There were hours and days and weeks of waiting, endless travel, bad food, bad weather, and close-quarters that made for immediate and long-lasting friendships. The rich fought alongside the poor; Christians bunked near Jews; Northerners marched side by side with Southerners. Men and women who otherwise might have never met found themselves depending upon each other for survival and companionship; for no matter what set them apart, the men and women of the American armed forces had one thing in common—they wanted victory and peace, and they wanted to go home.

ABOARD THE USS *LEXINGTON*—Personnel aboard the USS *Lexington* celebrate Christmas 1944 with makeshift decorations and a helmeted Santa Claus. *Photo U.S. Navy, Courtesy National Archives.*

SOMEWHERE IN AMERICA—A youngster hangs onto his soldier father while his parents embrace. The serviceman is one of the few who were lucky enough to be home for the holidays during wartime. *Photo Courtesy National Archives.*

To Members of the United States Army Expeditionary Forces:

You are a soldier of the United States Army. You have embarked for distant places where the war is being fought. Upon the outcome depends the freedom of your lives: the freedom of the lives of those you love—your fellow citizens—your people. Never were the enemies of freedom more tyrannical, more arrogant, more brutal. Yours is a God-fearing, proud, courageous people, which, throughout its history, has put its freedom under God before all other purposes. We who stay at home have our duties to perform—duties owed in many parts to you. You will be supported by the whole force and power of this nation. The victory you win will be a victory of all the people—common to them all.

You bear with you the hope, the confidence, the gratitude, and the prayers of your family, your fellow citizens, and your president—

Franklin Delano Roosevelt
The White House
March 1942

452ND SQUADRON, ANDREWS FIELD, BRAINTREE, ENGLAND—Salvo the Parachuting Dog has his rigging adjusted by 2nd Lieutenant Hugh R. Fletcher of Ohio and Technical Sergeant Glenn Shultz of California. Salvo, at right after a landing, made five successful jumps. *Photos U.S. Army, Courtesy National Archives.*

OKINAWA—With the luxury of a barbershop nowhere to be found, Private First Class Troy Dixon of Leadhill, Arkansas, uses a Japanese barber chair to cut the hair of Sergeant John Anderson of Anita, Pennsylvania, during a break in the fighting in June of 1945. *Photo Courtesy National Archives.*

SOMEWHERE IN EUROPE—A soldier faraway from his own family enjoys the admiration of a group of children. *Photo U.S. Army Signal Corps, Courtesy National Archives.*

ABOARD THE SS *PENNANT* ON THE WAY TO THE FRONT— Soldiers lie in their bunks aboard the troop transport ship after sailing from San Francisco in November 1942. Close quarters and shared experiences often meant close friendships, many of which continued long after the war. *Photo Courtesy National Archives.*

ABOARD THE USS *HARRIS*—Mr. Chips, a springer spaniel picked up by crew members of the USS *Harris*, shows his loyalty by wearing a hat made for him by his shipmates. Mr. Chips became the ship's mascot and participated in the attack on Attu. Loving sailors provided the spaniel with his own health record, identification card, and dog tags. *Photo U.S. Navy, Courtesy National Archives.*

THE SECRET WAR

Behind the tanks, ships, planes, and guns, behind the generals, admirals, soldiers, and sailors who fought the battles of World War II, was the secret world of military intelligence. Each decision, each move, and each risk was backed by the best information intelligence could provide, gathered with the aim of staying one step ahead of the enemy. Germany boasted of its unbreakable code, produced by the infamous Enigma machine; England relied upon "the man called Intrepid," super-spy William Stephenson. In America, the Office of War Information worked to undermine the morale of the enemy, the Office of Strategic Services sent 30,000 agents and spies on missions around the globe, and special groups like the Navajo Code Talkers developed coded language for the government's most valuable communications. Intelligence during World War II was a world shrouded in mystery, a world that to the everyday citizen seemed glamorous and exciting, and, by all accounts, a world without which the war could not have been won.

RADAR STATION SOMEWHERE IN ENGLAND—One of the first radar stations—a Fighter Direction Aerial System with a cabin mounted on the aerial structure that housed both the transmitter and receiver. *Photo Courtesy National Archives.*

Radar technology was still new at the beginning of World War II. The Germans discounted its usefulness to the British and made the decision not to bomb all of the twenty radar stations along the eastern and southeastern English coast in 1940, which left many stations intact to help the British Royal Air Force fight off the brutal bombing attack by the German Luftwaffe during the Battle of Britain. Ship radar was put into use a few years later, ending the German submarines' domination of the seas.

The Germans' Enigma machine was truly a masterpiece of military intelligence. Messages typed on a normal-appearing typewriter printed out in a complex code. The machine added another layer of deception with its ability to adjust itself after each entry, which guaranteed that the same letter typed two consecutive times would produce a different coded symbol. The Germans believed that the code they produced with their Enigma machine was unbreakable, but when the British captured one of the machines and deciphered its complex operation at the British Government Code and Cipher School at Bletchley Park in Bedfordshire, England, they had the ability to decipher top secret German communications. Entirely unbeknownst to the Germans, the British agents at Bletchley issued daily reports of enemy plans and movements. The reports that the British produced with their intercepted information were given to both the British High Command and the American generals under the code name Ultra.

LOCATION UNKNOWN—A highly classified Enigma machine developed by the Germans for secret communication during the war. *Photo Courtesy National Archives.*

*T*he Japanese were well schooled in the English language and proved quite adept at breaking American military code during the early months of World War II. On the advice of a missionary's son who had lived on a Navajo reservation, the Marines recruited Navajo men to help develop a code based on their unique, unwritten language. Navajo, spoken only by the tribes of the United States, had complex syntax and was nearly impossible to learn without extensive study and tutoring. The first Navajo Marine recruits, called Code Talkers, created a dictionary that combined existing Navajo words with new words created for certain military terms. Nearly 400 Navajos served in the Marine Corps as Code Talkers. The Navajo code lived up to all expectations and proved undecipherable to the Japanese. The accomplishment of these patriotic Americans was declassified and officially recognized in 1981, when President Ronald Reagan awarded them a Certificate of Appreciation.

BOUGAINVILLE IN THE SOUTH PACIFIC—Corporal Henry Bake, Jr., (left) and Private First Class George H. Kirk, Navajos serving with a Marine Signal Unit, operate a portable radio set in a clearing behind the front lines in 1943. *Photo U.S. Marine Corps, Courtesy National Archives.*

BALLARAT IN THE SOUTH PACIFIC—Privates First Class Preston Toledo and Frank Toledo, cousins and full-blooded Navajos who are attached to a Marine Artillery Regiment in the South Pacific, relay orders over a field radio in their native tongue in July 1943. *Photo U.S. Marine Corps, Courtesy National Archives.*

*A*mericans of Japanese descent played a vital role in military intelligence during World War II. More than 6,000 Japanese Americans served as interpreters and translators at the U.S. Army's Military Intelligence Service (MIS) Language School, and almost 4,000 went on to serve in combat, particularly in the Pacific theater. Their language abilities enabled them to interrogate Japanese prisoners, translate captured enemy documents, and more easily decipher enemy codes. A Japanese American intercepted the radio message that led to the successful attack on Japanese Admiral Yamamoto's plane and escorts in 1943; and a captured document containing Japan's master naval strategy in the central Pacific was translated by Japanese Americans from the MIS. In every branch of service, military leaders depended upon the specialized abilities of Japanese Americans for the crucial information only they were able to provide.

FIGHTING IN THE PACIFIC

In the summer of 1944, Allied forces began their final push toward the Japanese home islands. The path to Japan lay through the islands of the central and southwest Pacific—the Marianas, the Palaus, and the Philippines. These islands were necessary to provide a supply base and a launching point for an air attack. Led by Admirals Nimitz, Halsey, and King, the American Pacific Fleet, which had built up to nearly 5,000 vessels after the devastation of Pearl Harbor, included 600 warships and was strong and well prepared to do battle with Japan by sea. Through the summer, the Navy advanced toward Japan in the central Pacific through the islands of Saipan, Tinian, Guam, and Peleliu. In the southwest Pacific, General MacArthur led his forces through New Guinea and to Morotai Island. By September, the two forces were poised to converge in an invasion of the Philippines.

Marine forces under Admiral Nimitz landed on the island of Saipan, one of the Marianas, on June 15, 1944. The island, 3,000 miles west of Hawaii, was positioned to be a valuable base for the intended air assault on Japan. The Marines on Saipan fought fiercely and suffered heavy losses, but by July 10, the island was in American hands. In August of 1944, with fighting both on land and at sea, a combined Navy, Marine, and Army force gained control of the island of Guam.

PELELIU ISLAND— U.S. Marines move through the trenches on the beach at Peleliu on September 15, 1944. *Photo U.S. Marine Corps, Courtesy National Archives.*

Forty-five thousand Marines and soldiers fought on Peleliu Island, one of the Palaus, in the late summer and early autumn of 1944. In temperatures often as high as 115 degrees Fahrenheit, made worse by severe water shortages, the American troops fought a month-long battle and lost nearly 2,000 men before the island was secured.

BOUGAINVILLE—U.S. Marine Raiders use dogs for scenting the enemy and running messages while traveling toward the front lines in the jungle. *Photo U.S. Marine Corps, Courtesy National Archives.*

GUAM—Minutes after the U.S. Marines and Army assault troops landed on Guam on July 20, 1944, the United States flag is raised. *Photo U.S. Marine Corps, Courtesy National Archives.*

SAIPAN— A Marine private first class rests on an unexploded 16-inch mortar shell, July 4, 1944. *Photo U.S. Marine Corps, Courtesy National Archives.*

ON BOARD THE USS *SOUTH DAKOTA*— The men and crew of the *South Dakota* stand with bowed heads while Chaplain N. D. Lindner reads the benediction held in honor of fellow shipmates killed off Guam in the summer of 1944. *Photo U.S. Navy, Courtesy National Archives.*

While Admiral Nimitz was leading the advance through the Marianas toward Japan, General MacArthur moved his men northwest from Australia, through New Guinea, to Morotai, which would be his base for the invasion of the Philippines, the last stop before Japan. MacArthur, after fierce fighting on New Guinea, landed almost unopposed on Morotai.

KWAJALEIN ISLAND IN THE MARSHALLS—Men of the 7th division use flame throwers to smoke Japanese soldiers from a block house. *Photo Courtesy National Archives.*

MacArthur Returns to the Philippines

In Darwin, Australia, in March of 1942, General Douglas MacArthur uttered the words for which he would always be remembered. "The president of the United States ordered me to break through the Japanese lines," MacArthur declared, "and proceed from Corregidor to Australia for the purpose, as I understand, of organizing the American offensive against Japan, a primary purpose of which is the relief of the Philippines. I came through and I shall return." For the next two and one half years, MacArthur worked to fulfill that promise. He led Ameri-can and Australian forces in the defense of the Australian continent and in battles on New Guinea. From there he prepared for the advance to the Philippines. Flamboyant, handsome, the very picture of the American general, MacArthur was a World War I hero and, by this time, supreme commander of Allied forces in the Southwest Pacific. He was a bold and determined leader. The scene MacArthur left behind in the Philippines in 1942 was one of defeat and despair; his return in the autumn of 1944 was a personal, a professional, and a national redemption.

After wading ashore at Leyte, in the Philippines, in late October of 1944, MacArthur declared, "People of the Philippines, I have returned." But the struggle was far from over. The Battle of Leyte Gulf would go on for three days and involve both land and sea forces. Supported by Admiral William F. "Bull" Halsey's 3rd Fleet, MacArthur's men finally secured the island of Leyte on October 27.

After victory on Leyte, MacArthur led his men to the island of Luzon and its city of Manila. The first landings on Luzon took place on January 9, 1945; by March, Manila was free, as were nearly 5,000 Allied prisoners held there. Corregidor, the sight of General Wainwright's heroic stand and eventual capture after MacArthur's departure in May of 1942, was retaken by American forces in late February. All of the Philippine Islands were declared liberated on July 5, 1945.

LEYTE ISLAND, PHILIPPINES—After his landing crafts stopped short of the shore line, MacArthur wades ashore at Leyte. *Photo Courtesy National Archives.*

Duty-Honor-Country.

The soldier, above all other men, is required to practice the greatest act of religious training—sacrifice. In battle and in the face of danger and death, he discloses those divine attributes which his Maker gave when He created man in His own image. No physical courage and no brute instinct can take the place of the divine help which alone can sustain him....

And through all this welter of change and development, your mission remains fixed, determined, inviolable—it is to win our wars. Everything else in your professional career is but a corollary to this vital dedication...Yours is the profession of arms—the will to win, the sure knowledge that in war there is no substitute for victory; that if you lose, the nation will be destroyed; that the very obsession of your public service must by Duty-Honor-Country.

You stand as the nation's war guardian, as its lifeguard from the raging tides of international conflict, as its gladiator in the arena of battle. For a century and a half you have defended, guarded, and protected its hallowed tradition of liberty and freedom, of right and justice. Let civilian voices argue the merits or demerits of our processes of government...These great national problems are not for your professional participation or military solution. Your guidepost stands out like a ten-fold beacon in the night—Duty-Honor-Country.

The long Grey Line has never failed us. Were you to do so, a million ghosts in olive drab, in brown khaki, in blue and gray, would rise from their white crosses thundering those magic words—Duty-Honor-Country.

The soldier, above all other people, prays for peace, for he must suffer and bear the deepest wounds and scars of war. But always in our ears ring the ominous words of Plato, that wisest of all philosophers: "Only the dead has seen the end of War."

The shadows are lengthening for me. The twilight is here. My days of old have vanished tone and tint; they have gone glimmering through the dreams of things that were. Their memory is one of wondrous beauty, watered by tears, and coaxed and caressed by the smiles of yesterday.

I listen vainly, but with thirsty ear, for the witching melody of faint bugles blowing reveille, of far drums beating the long roll. In my dreams I hear again the crash of guns, the rattle of musketry, the strange, mournful mutter of the battlefield.

But in the evening of my memory, always I come back to West Point. Always there echoes and re-echoes Duty-Honor-Country.

Today marks my final roll call with you, but I want you to know that when I cross the river, my last conscious thought will be The Corps—and The Corps—and The Corps—and The Corps.

I bid you farewell.

General Douglas MacArthur
West Point, New York
May 12, 1962

LEYTE, PHILIPPINES—General MacArthur surveys the beachhead on Leyte. With his familiar corncob pipe, regal bearing, and articulate speeches, MacArthur instilled confidence in his men as well as in the American people; few military leaders have been as revered and loved as he. *Photo Courtesy National Archives.*

MOROTAI ISLAND—General Douglas MacArthur (inside circle) stands surrounded by GIs at the sight of the first American flag to fly over Morotai Island on September 15, 1944. *Photo U.S. Navy, Courtesy National Archives.*

*U*ntil 1942, MacArthur's headquarters was on Fort Corregidor, on an island in Manila Bay, off the Bataan Peninsula in the Philippines. When it was overrun by the Japanese, MacArthur fled from Corregidor by submarine. Because MacArthur (for sound military reasons) spent his time in the relative safety of Corregidor Island, his men on the Bataan Peninsula, who realized they were slated for captivity or death, nicknamed him Dugout Doug.

Iwo Jima

The island of Iwo Jima is eight square miles of volcanic rock and ash located 660 miles southeast of Tokyo, between the Mariana Islands and Japan. Although with the Marianas and the Philippines in hand the Allies could launch air attacks on Japan's home islands, more than 20,000 Japanese soldiers were in place on Iwo Jima, perfectly situated to shoot down Allied planes before they reached their target. In mid-February of 1945, a combined American Navy and Marine force led an assault on Iwo Jima, landing on the island's steep beaches just before 9:00 on the morning of February 19. The ascent up the steep, sandy beaches was slow and difficult, but the fiercest fighting lay ahead on Mt. Suribachi on the island's southern end. In a network of tunnels and bunkers built within Suribachi, the Japanese took refuge and mounted a tenacious defense. The battle to flush them out and take the mountain was won on February 23, 1945. On that date, the American flag was finally raised on Suribachi's summit, creating one of the most memorable and inspiring scenes of the war. Fighting on Iwo Jima continued, however, until late March, when the island was finally secured.

IN A FOXHOLE ON IWO JIMA—Private First Class Rez P. Hester of the 7th War Dog Platoon of the 25th Regiment sleeps under the watchful eye of his Doberman pinscher, Butch, in February of 1945. *Photo U.S. Marine Corps, Courtesy National Archives.*

*T*he Seabees, or Navy construction battalions, built the airfields, bridges, roads, and camps for American and Allied troops. Secretary of the Navy James Forrestal said of these dedicated men, "The Seabees carried the war in the Pacific on their backs."

IWO JIMA—CBs of 50th Battalion sit on sandbags in a chapel and bow their heads in prayer during candlelight Holy Communion service. *Photo U.S. Navy, Courtesy National Archives.*

OFF THE COAST OF IWO JIMA—Amphibious personnel carriers jammed with Marines speed toward the assault beach on southeastern Iwo Jima. Nearly 500 vessels took part in the Iwo Jima campaign. *Photo U.S. Marine Corps, Courtesy National Archives.*

*A*llied forces prepared for the attack on Iwo Jima with more than seventy days of bombing meant to weaken the Japanese defenses in preparation for the landing of troops. The Japanese, however, retreated to their bunkers inside Mt. Suribachi and were still able to mount a strong defense when the full attack commenced. Casualties on both sides were very high; nearly 7,000 Americans lost their lives and nearly 15,000 were injured.

MT. SURIBACHI, IWO JIMA—Battle weary Marines kneel while a Catholic chaplain celebrates mass before a makeshift altar on the littered slopes of Mt. Suribachi, after the men had cleared the volcano of its Japanese defenders. Two Marines wearing camouflaged helmets hold a poncho to protect the candles, chalice, and Bible from the wind. *Photo Courtesy National Archives.*

*L*ieutenant General Holland M. "Howling Mad" Smith called the fighting on Iwo Jima the "toughest the Marines had run across in 168 years." Tough fighting, however, brought out a heroic display of bravery. Twenty-seven Medals of Honor were bestowed upon American soldiers for their actions on Iwo Jima.

ON THE SUMMIT OF MT. SURIBACHI, IWO JIMA— Marines of the U.S. 5th Division raise the American flag on the scarred summit of newly captured Mt. Suribachi on Iwo Jima. The Marines immediately recognized the symbolic value of the flag and took it down for preservation, replacing it with another. The flag raising, although recognized by every American as a symbol of victory, was far from the end of the battle. More than two weeks of fighting remained before March 13, 1945, the date on which U.S. Fleet Admiral Chester Nimitz proclaimed the suspension of Japanese rule on the island. *Photo Courtesy National Archives.*

THE ORDEAL OF THE USS FRANKLIN

The carrier USS *Franklin* was part of Task Force 58, a group given the responsibility of striking the Japanese home islands as the main Allied forces closed in on Japan in the early months of 1945. The Japanese navy was by this time severely weakened; its defenses had come down to kamikaze pilots and bold dive bombers who assaulted Allied ships as they sailed ever closer to the Japanese homeland. It was one such dive bomber that landed two blows on the flight deck of the *Franklin* in March of 1945. The *Franklin* may well have survived the blow relatively unscathed if not for the freshly fueled planes lined up on the gasoline-soaked flight deck. The bombs ignited the fuel and set off a day-long series of explosions that spread fire throughout the ship. Of the 3,000 men aboard, 724 were killed and 265 were wounded; it was the worst single disaster in U.S. naval history. But the *Franklin*'s tragedy was met by unprecedented bravery on the part of her crew. One Medal of Honor, nineteen Navy Crosses, twenty-two Silver Stars, 115 Bronze Stars, and 234 Letters of Commendation were awarded to her men. The fires aboard the *Franklin* were eventually extinguished, and the ship returned to America, but the heroism and bravery of the men aboard will be remembered forever.

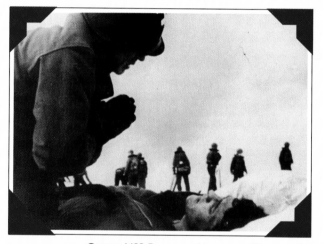

OFF THE USS *FRANKLIN*—The *Franklin* suffers smoke and flames after an attack by a Japanese dive bomber. Unlike the Japanese kamikaze pilots, the flyers aboard these dive bombers had every intention of returning safely from their attacks. *Photo U.S. Navy, Courtesy National Archives.*

ON THE USS *FRANKLIN*—Lieutenant Commander Joseph O'Callahan, Navy chaplain, administers the last rites to an injured crewman aboard the USS *Franklin*. O'Callahan maintained his composure and showed unbelievable courage and strength during the ordeal of the *Franklin*. The forty-year-old Boston native—who prided himself on his camaraderie with the men aboard ship—administered last rites, offered comfort and first aid to the wounded, fought fires, and even helped carry the ship's supply of unexploded five-inch shells to the deck to be thrown overboard before the fire reached them. O'Callahan, who had suffered a shrapnel wound in an early explosion, continued to work tirelessly throughout the day. Months later, he tried unsuccessfully to lift a single five-inch shell. In the face of disaster, he had found truly extraordinary courage and strength. O'Callahan was awarded the Congressional Medal of Honor for his bravery above and beyond the call of duty. *Photo U.S. Navy, Courtesy National Archives.*

BROOKLYN HARBOR, NEW YORK—The officers and men who survived the Japanese attack on the USS *Franklin* proudly stand at attention on the flight deck as the ship enters her home port. *Photo U.S. Navy, Courtesy National Archives.*

THE BATTLE FOR OKINAWA

Sixty times larger than Iwo Jima and defended by as many as 100,000 Japanese, the island of Okinawa was the last stop on the way to Japan for Allied forces. It lay only 325 miles south of the Japanese island of Kyushu. The United States 10th Army, made up of Army and Marine divisions, landed almost unopposed on Okinawa on April 1, 1945. The Japanese had decided to let the attackers take the northern part of the island while the Japanese tight-ened their grip on the southern third. Hoping to lull the Americans into a false sense of security, the Japanese waited. But on May 4, they launched a massive counteroffensive. The resulting battle was deadly, and both sides suffered terrible casualties. At sea, the Navy support fleet fell victim to a series of kamikaze attacks. Not until June 22 did organized Japanese resistance cease on Okinawa; by that time the combined death toll was well over 100,000.

OKINAWA—U.S. Marines, following the rapid Japanese retreat, pause for a moment of rest at the base of a Japanese war memorial on April 12, 1945. *Photo U.S. Navy, Courtesy National Archives.*

When the American forces originally landed on Okinawa, the Japanese were nowhere to be seen; their leaders, holed up in Shuri Castle, a fifteenth century fort on the island's southern end, had decided that to defend the entire island was impossible. They pinned their hopes on a tight and persistent defense in the south, where the steep ridges and difficult terrain would slow American movement.

OKINAWA—The 29th Marine tank-borne infantry moves to take the town of Ghuta on Okinawa on April 1, 1945. *Photo U.S. Marine Corps, Courtesy National Archives.*

A Marine described the landing on Okinawa as like he had "stepped into a fairy tale." The countryside, dotted with fields of barley and wildflowers, was beautiful, and the lack of Japanese resistance was surprising and welcome. But, as would later be noted, the landing happened on April Fool's Day; the peace that greeted the Marines would soon be revealed as part of a careful strategy of deception.

WOMEN IN UNIFORM

Approximately 265,000 women enlisted in the armed service of the United States during World War II, each one a volunteer. Opportunities for women in the military were extremely limited in 1941, and opposition to their presence in the armed forces ran high in American society. But as the war wore on, women proved themselves an asset in every area in which they were granted involve-ment, and attitudes and restrictions began to soften. During World War II, women held the traditional clerical and office positions, but also received such non-traditional assignments as pilots, truck drivers, mechanics, and techni-cians. American women were eager to serve; the only lim-its on their contribution to the war effort were those placed on their opportunities for service.

U.S. ARMY CAMP, GREAT BRITAIN—Before going to France, U.S. Army WACs take care of some basic housekeeping by cleaning their mess kits in boiling water. *Photo Courtesy National Archives.*

FORT HUACHUCA, ARIZONA—In December 1942, two WACs are servicing trucks after completing instruction at Fort Des Moines. *Photo Courtesy National Archives.*

Women found opportunities expand-ing for them through-out the war in each branch of service. The women's reserve of the Navy (WAVES) enlisted 100,000 women, and the Marine Corps Women's Reserve, which began in Febru-ary of 1943, twenty-three thousand. The Coast Guard began accepting women for duty during World War II as SPARS, some of whom had the unique opportunity of working with LORAN, or Long Range Aid to Navy, which sent radio sig-nals to ships at sea.

NEW YORK HARBOR—The U.S. Army's first all Puerto Rican Women's Army Corps unit, recruited in Puerto Rico and assigned to the Army Post Office of the New York Port of Embarkation, is escorted on a sightseeing tour of New York Harbor. *Photo Courtesy National Archives.*

The Women's Army Corps (WAC) began as the Women's Auxiliary Army Corps (WAAC), which was not an official part of the U.S. Army. In 1943, the name was changed, and the group officially attached to the Army. In all, 150,000 women served in the WAC, in positions from typists and switchboard oper-ators to truck drivers and mechan-ics. The WAC gave enlisted women the best chance for overseas duty—the Navy, Marines, and Coast Guard limited women to ser-vice in the U.S. Eight thousand WACs served in Europe, more than 5,000 in the Pacific, and hundreds in the China-India-Burma theater.

One of the largest groups of women in service were the Army and Navy nurses, many of whom served in the midst of battlefields across the globe. Sixty thousand nurses served in all; nearly 1,500 were decorated for bravery. Their courage and skills gave the Ameri-can public a new understanding of the crucial role of nurses in the medical community.

WOMEN'S AIR FORCE SERVICE PILOTS

In August of 1943, with World War II placing extreme demands on the pilots of the U.S. Army Air Corps, Jacqueline Cochran—a world-renowned racing pilot and the head of the Women's Flying Training Command, a group of nearly 2,000 women pilots trained to fly military aircraft across the country—was asked by the government to join her group with the Women's Auxiliary Ferrying Squadron to create the Women Air Force Service Pilots (WASP). The mission of the WASPs was to ferry military aircraft to pilots of the Army Air Corps, to test newly repaired planes, and to train antiaircraft gunners by acting as moving targets for practice. They were not, however, allowed to serve in combat or overseas. The WASPs flew from August 1943 until December 1944. Although they were never brought into the American military—the program was run under Civil Service—the WASPs lived and trained by military standards and military discipline. In the words of General Henry Arnold, the WASPs were "as much an integral part of the Army Air Force as their civil service status would permit.... Together with the women pilots of the Allies, the WASPs proved that women have the ability and the capacity to perform the most difficult jobs in flying." Despite Arnold's words of praise, however, the WASPs were disbanded in 1944 without having been accepted as part of the Army Air Corps. In 1949, retired WASPs were offered commissions in the newly founded United States Air Force, but were not assigned flying duties. It was not until 1977 that Congress acknowledged that the WASPs of World War II had indeed been military pilots. In that year, the WASPs were given honorary discharges and listed as veterans, and women were finally accepted into Air Force flight training. The women who fly for the United States Air Force today proudly trace their heritage back to Jackie Cochran and her WASP pilots who battled discrimination along with the normal hardships of wartime flying to open the skies to American women.

Jacqueline Cochran, Director of Women Pilots. *Photo U.S. Air Force, WASP Collection, Texas Woman's University.*

CAMP DAVIS ARMY AIRFIELD, NORTH CAROLINA—A WASP pilot and tow-reel operator, members of the 3rd Tow Target Squadron, 1st Air Force, in a Dauntless A-24 dive bomber are on a tow target mission in the fall of 1943. *Photo U.S. Air Force, WASP Collection, Texas Woman's University.*

CAMP DAVIS ARMY AIRFIELD, NORTH CAROLINA— Women Air Force Service Pilots head for their planes. *Photo U.S. Air Force, Courtesy National Archives.*

MAIL CALL

For soldiers and sailors far away from friends and family, the only reliable contact with home was the mail. During the war years, millions of letters were written and millions more received by the men and women of the armed forces. So great was the volume of mail that the government devised V-Mail, a miniaturized, self-contained letter and envelope that was lightweight and guaranteed to reach its destination in under ten days. Writing letters filled empty hours and helped relieve the boredom of military life; one soldier reportedly wrote at least three and as many as nine letters home to his wife every single day of his tour of duty. Receiving letters and the coveted packages of magazines, books, and food brightened the darkest day. The prolific letter writing abilities of the soldiers placed a heavy burden on the censors, who were required to read every word and line of each letter before it was sent and delete any information deemed a threat to national security. To the censors and the post offices, the volume of mail was a daily problem; to the soldiers and their families, it was a lifeline.

A NAVY HOSPITAL IN THE SOUTH PACIFIC—U. S. Navy nurses receive their first package from home. It contains books, candy, and pajamas—all very welcome items. A survey of military personnel found that the most popular packages contained magazines, fruitcakes, and sausage. *Photo U.S. Navy, Courtesy National Archives.*

SOMEWHERE OVERSEAS—An elated Coastguardsman opens a V-Mail letter. The government devised V-Mail to ease the burden created by the vast and unprecedented volume of mail produced by World War II. *Photo Courtesy National Archives.*

ON THE DOCK AT PEARL HARBOR—The enormous task of distributing a sailor's mail fell to the fleet post office. Below, stacks of mail await delivery in August of 1945. *Photo Courtesy National Archives.*

The mention of World War II brings back a flood of memories of my childhood. I had an uncle, my mother's brother Soto, who joined the Army shortly before December of 1941; knowing that he was involved put a human face on the war for our family. Only ten years old, I could not truly understand the significance of the war and its complex issues; I knew only that it was serious and that my Uncle Soto was a part of it all. I remember sitting on the living room floor with my three sisters—long before television came into our home—listening to the radio reports of the attack on Pearl Harbor. To a child, the reports, although serious and frightening, also contained an element of excitement; after all, the war was far away, and what did a ten-year-old boy know of fear and death and tragedy?

My uncle spent the next three years in North Africa and Europe, and our family kept a daily watch on events in those distant places as if our attention would help keep him safe. We followed the daily maps in the papers that tracked the progress of Allied troops and sometimes—like in the Battle of the Bulge—the progress of the enemy. It was almost like a game, watching and waiting to see if our troops would meet up with the Russian troops in their advance toward Germany.

We waited every day for the mail to come to see if there was a letter from Uncle Soto; when he did write, we would read his words aloud, glad to know he was alive and well. We went through the worry during the invasion of North Africa, Italy, and finally, Normandy—each time the letter came telling us he had survived. Uncle Soto was awarded the Purple Star two times, and he finally came home after the final victory in 1945. I remember the victory parade through town on V-E Day when victory in Europe was assured. People gathered in the streets cheering and blowing horns. Church bells were ringing, and for a moment it seemed we had all forgotten that there was still a war on in the Pacific against the Japanese. For all of us on the home front, even those with loved ones fighting overseas, it was hard to understand the reality of what the war meant. Fifty years later, I look back on those childhood days with an almost romantic fascination.

Peter Skarmeas

SOMEWHERE IN THE PACIFIC—Coastguardsmen on a troop transport pack the number three hatch as mail call promises precious words from home. For many families at home, letters were the only concrete assurance that their loved ones were, at least for the time being, safe and sound. *Photo U.S. Coast Guard, Courtesy National Archives.*

ICELAND—Christmas mail is distributed to the men at the outpost base. *Photo U.S. Coast Guard, Courtesy National Archives.*

HEROES AT SEA: CAPTAIN GALLERY AND U-BOAT 505

Winston Churchill once said that "the only thing which really frightened me during the war was the U-boat peril." Churchill was right to be worried. The German *Unterseeboot*, or U-boat, inflicted severe damage on Allied shipping during the early years of the war in the Atlantic. In one eight-month period in 1941, U-boats sank more than 300 merchant ships and seriously threatened the flow of supplies to the British Isles. The tide began to turn in 1942 as improved sonar and the advent of ship radar made detection of the U-boats easier, but the U-boat remained a potent symbol of the German menace. American forces captured only one U-boat during World War II. Captain Daniel V. Gallery, Jr., and his men took the German U-boat *505* off the coast of the Cape Verde Islands on June 4, 1944; it was the first enemy warship captured by the United States Navy since the War of 1812. The capture provided naval intelligence with valuable German code books, and the heroism of Gallery and his men gave a boost to American morale in every theater of the war.

ON BOARD THE GERMAN U-BOAT *505*—A smiling Captain Gallery stands in the conning tower of the captured German submarine that now displays the message "Can Do Junior." *Photo U.S. Navy, Courtesy National Archives.*

Captain Daniel Gallery, commander of the USS Guadalcanal, was patrolling the waters off the Cape Verde Islands in June of 1944 along with five destroyer escorts when he detected the underwater presence of a German U-boat in the area. Gallery alerted his men and ordered one of the destroyers to depth-charge the German submarine. Taken by surprise, the crew of the U-boat brought their sub to the surface and abandoned ship. The men of one of the destroyers, who were well schooled by Captain Gallery, quickly boarded the sub, disconnected the demolition charges the fleeing Germans had set, and seized the ship's code books. The sub was then taken in tow by the Guadalcanal and brought to Bermuda. After the war, German U-boat 505 became a permanent exhibit at the Museum of Science and Industry in Chicago, Illinois.

ABOARD THE USS *GUADALCANAL*—The Stars and Stripes flutter from the conning tower of the captured Nazi U-boat 505. *Photo U.S. Navy, Courtesy National Archives.*

The men under the command of Captain Gallery were trained with a special emphasis on recovering coding books and devices from damaged or captured subs. The documents and equipment they seized from U-boat 505 were extremely helpful to the U.S. Navy in decoding German Enigma communications. Captain Gallery was promoted to rear admiral in December of 1945. He retired from the military in 1960 to pursue a successful career as a writer.

HEROES AT SEA: THE FIGHTING SULLIVANS

The five Sullivan brothers from Waterloo, Iowa, joined the Navy at the outset of World War II and requested assignment to the same ship. In one of the war's great tragedies, all five Sullivans were among the 700 men to lose their lives when their ship, the USS *Juneau*, went down during the Battle of Guadalcanal. In response to the tragedy, the Navy issued a new regulation forbidding relatives from serving aboard the same ship. After their deaths, the five Sullivan brothers were the subject of a popular 1944 motion picture, *The Fighting Sullivans*. The movie was a tribute to their sacrifice and patriotism and was symbolic of similar sacrifices made by young men and women throughout America and the world during the Second World War.

At left, a poster of the Sullivan brothers was used for patriotic and promotional enlistment efforts; at right are the Sullivan brothers aboard their ship, the USS *Juneau. Photos Courtesy National Archives.*

I was only eight years old when World War II began, but I soon understood a little of what war truly meant. The twelfth of thirteen children, I had five sisters and seven older brothers, three of whom were old enough to serve; all three volunteered. Steve and John went to the Army and were involved in several European battle zones. Charlie joined the Navy and was sent to the Pacific. They were so young, and we were frightened for them and sad to see them leave; but they were also brave, and we were proud of their courage and their sacrifice.

The radio and newspapers and movie newsreels kept our family as up-to-date as they could on what was happening, but the daily reminders in our home made the most solemn impression on me. On our parlor wall hung a beautiful collage of my brothers' official portraits in uniform, along with patriotic symbols and sayings. They looked so grown-up and so much older in their uniforms; I was very much in awe of my big brothers. Another patriotic reminder hung in our family's window and announced to people passing by that we had loved ones fighting in the war. This same symbol—a small satin rectangle with a blue star on a white background, bordered in red and trimmed in gold braid and fringe—was visible in so many windows up and down the streets of our neighborhood. Our banner had three blue stars for my three brothers; friends and neighbors sadly had to replace a blue star with a gold one when a loved one was killed in battle, but their banners still hung proudly in memory of a patriot. My family was blessed—our boys came home, war-weary and old beyond their years, but safe and sound. They were more aware than any of us of the price sometimes necessary to protect and defend the freedom we so often take for granted.

Mary Theodore

HEROES IN THE AIR: THE MEMPHIS BELLE

When Lieutenant Robert K. Morgan was assigned his first B-17 bomber as a member of the U.S. Army Air Corps during World War II, in keeping with tradition, he chose a name for his plane. He called her the *Memphis Belle*. Morgan could not have imagined that the name of his aircraft would soon be known in every corner of America. Morgan and the *Memphis Belle* compiled an impressive record during their tour of duty in 1942-43. The *Memphis Belle* was credited with destroying eight German planes and was one of the first American aircraft to complete twenty-five missions over Europe. Despite coming under heavy fire on several occasions, Morgan brought his crew home safely from each mission. But it was the story of her name that made the *Memphis Belle* truly famous. Before leaving for Europe, Morgan had become engaged to a young woman named Margaret Polk. When Morgan went off to war in 1942, Margaret waited for him at her parents' home in Memphis, Tennessee. The name painted on the nose of Morgan's B-17, along with the accompanying paint-

ing of a beautiful woman, was a tribute to his own Memphis belle back home, his fiancée Margaret. The story of the heroic, dashing, young pilot and his devoted fiancée proved irresistible to the American people; Morgan's flying exploits were recounted across the nation, and he and Margaret soon became a celebrity couple. Recognizing good propaganda, the War Department enlisted Morgan and the *Memphis Belle* to participate in a national publicity tour upon his return to America. After a brief reunion in Memphis, Morgan and Polk were separated once more as the pilot and his plane went on tour. In city after city, Morgan and the *Memphis Belle* drew large, enthusiastic crowds, raising money and inspiring patriotism. Unfortunately, the tour kept Morgan away from Memphis and away from Margaret; within months the engagement was called off. But the legend of the *Memphis Belle* proved more durable than the facts behind it. What the public remembered was not the broken engagement, but the heroic pilot, the devoted fiancée, and the plane that bore her name.

The B-17 bomber, known as the "Flying Fortress," was a rugged plane, heavily armed and armored and built to stand up to a barrage of enemy fire. The Memphis Belle herself was proof of the B-17's durability. Nine times Lieutenant Morgan lost an engine during a flight and still managed to finish his mission. On one flight he lost a section of the plane's tail and on another an enemy hit tore a gaping hole in the Belle's right wing. But Morgan was as tough as his Flying Fortress. In the words of one of his devoted crew members, "He always brought us home." Although he later flew the B-29, considered by many to be a superior aircraft to the B-17, Morgan remained forever loyal to the Flying Fortress and insisted to the end that it was the best plane he ever flew.

MEMPHIS, TENNESSEE—Captain Morgan, embracing Margaret Polk, and his crew pose in front of the *Memphis Belle*. *Photo Courtesy Memphis Belle Memorial Assoc. Inc.*

MEMPHIS, TENNESSEE—A photograph autographed by Robert Morgan shows the crew of the *Memphis Belle*. *Photo Courtesy Memphis Belle Memorial Assoc. Inc.*

The War Department, so anxious to make the romance between Lieutenant Morgan and Margaret Polk work for American morale, may well have had a hand in the relationship's premature end. Although Morgan and Polk had planned to be married shortly after he returned from Europe, tour organizers convinced them to postpone the wedding until the Belle had completed the rounds of American cities; in the organizers' view, the romantic story had more appeal with an engaged couple than with a husband and wife. Morgan and his fiancée obliged; but as the months on the road wore on, they found the distance between them growing. Before the tour was completed, the wedding was called off. Morgan rebounded quickly, however. Within months, he had signed on for a second tour of duty in the Pacific and had married a woman named Dorothy from his home state of North Carolina. Morgan returned to war flying a new plane, a B-29, with a new name painted on its nose—the Dauntless Dottie—in honor of his wife.

THE END OF THE NIGHTMARE IN EUROPE

General Dwight D. Eisenhower issued a short but monumental message from his headquarters in Rheims, France, in the first week of May 1945. "The mission of this Allied force was fulfilled at 0241 local time, May 7, 1945." Berlin had fallen; Germany had surrendered. The war in Europe was over. V-E Day came just short of a year after the Allied landing at Normandy. In the eleven months between June 1944 and May 1945, long, hard battles had been fought, and the true horror of the Nazi regime had finally begun to emerge. The formal documents of surrender were signed on May 8. Adolph Hitler was not present; he had committed suicide on April 30 rather than face surrender. In the weeks and months ahead, the celebration of victory would be tempered by the reality of a continuing war with Japan and by the daily revelations of the war's terrible toll on the people of Europe and the world.

GERMANY—A Russian soldier hugs an American soldier as the two nations' forces meet each other during the Allied advance. *Photo U.S. Signal Corps, Courtesy National Archives.*

ON THE ROAD IN HOLLAND—In September 1944, American troops encounter a horsecart of evacuees ordered from their Dutch hometown. Across Europe, civilians were displaced from their homes; cities and towns were destroyed; and families were torn apart. V-E Day was a day of joy, but the hard work of recovery was just beginning. *Photo U.S. Signal Corps, Courtesy National Archives.*

ON THE RAILROAD OUT OF GERMANY—Jewish youngsters make their way to Palestine after being liberated from the Buchenwald concentration camp. The girl on the left is from Poland, the boy in the center is from Latvia, and the girl on the right is from Hungary. *Photo U.S. Signal Corps, Courtesy National Archives.*

The Nazis' "final and unalterably uncompromising solution," the systematic destruction of the Jewish people of Europe, was reported in the press as early as 1933. The New York Times stated in October of 1941 that the "complete elimination of Jews from European life appears to be a fixed German policy." Nonetheless, much of the world seemed unable to comprehend the reality or the atrocity of Hitler's plan until after the fall of the Third Reich. It was then that American and other Allied soldiers saw with their own eyes the concentration camps where six million Jews and as many as six million others were tortured and executed. General Eisenhower and other leaders encouraged the soldiers to tour the liberated camps, to take photos, to remember, and to tell the world what they saw at places called Dachau, Auschwitz, Treblinka, Buchenwald, and Belsen. The war had indeed been won in Europe, but the violent inhumanity of the Nazi regime had left a permanent scar upon the continent and the world.

HARRY S TRUMAN

Until he served as chairman of the Special Committee to Investigate the National Defense Program in the late 1930s, Senator Harry Truman was little known, either inside or outside Washington. His work on that committee earned him notice; still, it was a surprise to many when President Roosevelt accepted Harry Truman as his vice-presidential running mate in 1944. It was an even greater shock less than six months after the election when Roosevelt died and Harry S Truman became the president of the United States. Roosevelt had been in office for more than twelve years; for many Americans he was the only president they could remember. Now an unknown, plain-spoken man from Missouri had the fate of the nation—and of the world—in his hands. Truman himself recognized the burden that fell so suddenly and squarely on his shoulders on April 12, 1945, the day Franklin Roosevelt died. "I felt," Truman remarked, "like the moon, the stars, and all the planets had fallen on me." In a matter of months, Truman would be in Potsdam meeting with British Prime Minister Winston Churchill and Russian Premier Josef Stalin, faced with decisions that would truly change the course of history.

ABOARD THE USS *AUGUSTA* EN ROUTE TO THE POTSDAM CONFERENCE—President Harry S Truman shares a meal with sailors. Truman, as a World War I veteran, had a special affinity for the men in uniform. *Photo U.S. Navy, Courtesy National Archives.*

ON THE DECK OF THE USS *AUGUSTA*—President Truman and Secretary of State Jimmy Byrnes take a bearing on another ship that is steaming ahead. *Photo U.S. Navy, Courtesy National Archives.*

ON THE DECK OF THE USS *AUGUSTA*—President Truman and Secretary of State Byrnes wave to the British destroyer that greets their arrival in Europe. The *Augusta* was the same ship that carried President Roosevelt to his first meeting with Winston Churchill in 1941 off the coast of Canada. *Photo U.S. Navy, Courtesy National Archives.*

POTSDAM, GERMANY—President Truman with British Prime Minister Winston Churchill at the "Little White House" in July 1945. *Photo Courtesy National Archives.*

LITTLE ROCK, ARKANSAS—President Truman marches with members of Battery D, 35th Infantry Division, in a parade honoring World War II veterans in June 1949. *Photo U.S. Signal Corps, Courtesy National Archives.*

*T*he trip to Potsdam was the first European travel for Harry Truman since his days in World War I. Truman had been president for only three months at the time, and he had to prove to Americans at home and to the leaders of a watching world that he had the confidence and skill to lead the nation during wartime. At Potsdam, President Truman told Josef Stalin of America's new atomic bomb. Although the Russian leader expressed surprise at Truman's news, Russian intelligence had already informed him of the American weapon. In this case, Stalin was better informed than the president; Truman had learned of the atomic bomb only after taking the oath of office.

THE MANHATTAN PROJECT

In 1939, President Franklin Roosevelt gave his approval to the Manhattan Engineering District—the code name for the American efforts to create an atomic weapon. Roosevelt's approval of the Manhattan Project, as it became known, was in large part due to a letter sent to him by a group of scientists, including Albert Einstein, that warned of German progress in the area of atomic research and urged the United States to step up its efforts to produce the world's first atomic bomb. Drawing on the best minds of science and the leaders of industry, the Manhattan Project achieved its goal on July 15, 1945, when the first successful test bomb was detonated at the bombing range in Alamogordo, 200 miles south of Los Alamos, New Mexico. Its detonation prompted J. Robert Oppenheimer, one of its creators, to quote an ominous line: "I am become Death, the shatterer of worlds."

LOS ALAMOS, NEW MEXICO—A refugee from fascist Italy, Enrico Fermi won the Nobel Prize in 1938 and was assigned to the atomic bomb laboratory in Los Alamos after his 1942 success with nuclear reaction at Chicago. *Photo Courtesy National Archives.*

In December of 1942, government officials in Washington received a cryptic telegram from the Chicago headquarters of the American Atomic Energy Program. "The Italian Navigator," the telegram declared, "has just landed in the New World." The telegram referred to Italian scientist Enrico Fermi, who had just completed the first self-sustaining nuclear chain reaction—a vital step on the road to the atomic bomb.

TRENTON, NEW JERSEY—Albert Einstein, his daughter Margot Einstein, and his secretary Helene Dukas take the oath of citizenship in the Federal building on October 1, 1940. *Photo Wide World Photos, Courtesy National Archives.*

OAK RIDGE, TENNESSEE—As part of the Manhattan Project, a secret government-operated plant was built in this southern city. *Photo Courtesy National Archives.*

Albert Einstein came to the United States in the 1930s to escape Hitler's regime in Germany. He accepted a position at Princeton's Institute for Advanced Study, where he continued his pioneering work in physics. In 1939, Einstein added his name to the letter that convinced President Roosevelt to approve the Manhattan Project. Einstein's work was the foundation for the atomic research of the 30s and 40s, and he recognized the power and destruction promised by atomic weaponry. As a native German, he also understood the terrible potential of such a weapon in the hands of a man like Adolph Hitler. A gentle, peace-loving man, Einstein was deeply troubled by the ethical implications of atomic science. He once remarked, "I made one great mistake in my life, when I signed the letter to Franklin Roosevelt."

Top secret weapons plants were operated in Oak Ridge, Tennessee; Los Alamos, New Mexico; and in Washington State. So compartmentalized and top secret was production at these plants that of the nearly 600,000 workers who toiled inside, only a very few had knowledge of their finished product.

ENDING THE WAR

"Let there be no mistake about it," President Harry S Truman remarked about his decision to use the atomic bomb on Japan in August of 1945, "I regarded the bomb as a military weapon and never had any doubt that it should be used." The alternative was Operation Olympic, the planned Allied land invasion of Japan. Estimates put the number of men needed for such an invasion at one million; General George Marshall told President Truman to expect close to a quarter of a million Americans to lose their lives in fighting on the Japanese home islands. In all of World War II, not a single Japanese unit had surrendered; even in the face of certain defeat, the people of Japan would fight to the last man in defense of their homeland. A land invasion, all agreed, promised victory only after a long, deadly fight. With the full agreement of the Allied leaders gathered at Potsdam, Harry Truman approved the atomic bomb as the best military option available. The objective was not the destruction of Japan, but its surrender, and the immediate end of World War II.

Having found the bomb we have used it. . . . We have used it against those who attacked us without warning at Pearl Harbor, against those who have starved and beaten and executed American prisoners of war, against those who have abandoned all pretense of obeying international laws of warfare. We have used it in order to shorten the agony of war, in order to save the lives of thousands and thousands of young Americans. We shall continue to use it until we completely destroy Japan's power to make war. Only a Japanese surrender will stop us.

President Harry S Truman
August 9, 1945

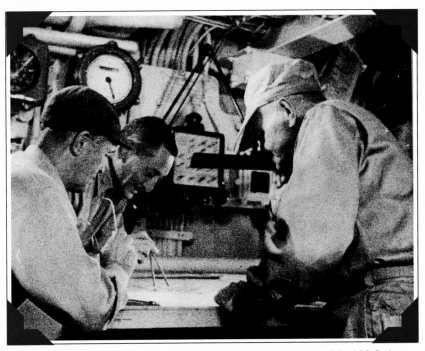

Aboard the USS *Enterprise*—Admiral William Halsey, commander of the U.S. 3rd Fleet, gathers with the members of his staff on July 30, 1945, to map out the bombardment of the Japanese homeland. *Photo U.S. Navy, Courtesy National Archives.*

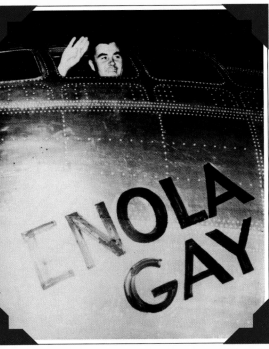

Unknown Airfield—Colonel Paul W. Tibbets, Jr., the pilot of the *Enola Gay*, the plane that dropped the atomic bomb on Hiroshima, waves from his cockpit before takeoff on August 6, 1945. *Photo U.S. Air Force, Courtesy National Archives.*

The atomic bomb delivered upon Hiroshima on August 6, 1945, by the American B-29 Enola Gay killed an estimated 80,000 Japanese instantly and as many as 50,000 more over the next several months; all but 10,000 of the dead were civilians. Scientists who worked on the bomb had estimated a death toll of near 20,000. When the Japanese refused to surrender, a second bomb was dropped, this one by the B-29 Bockscar on August 9, 1945, on the city of Nagasaki, where 70,000 Japanese lost their lives. On August 14, 1945, the Japanese agreed to an unconditional surrender. The atomic bomb brought an end to World War II, but it also ushered in a new and frightening era in world history. The devastation caused by these bombs was unlike anything the world had ever seen. In the words of President Truman, man had harnessed "the force from which the sun draws its power." It was, he acknowledged, "an awful responsibility." The advances of science had, in 1945, raised the stakes of human conflict to a terrifying level.

The historic fact remains and must not be judged in the after-time, that the decision whether or not to use the atomic bomb to compel the surrender of Japan was never an issue. There was unanimous, automatic, unquestioned agreement around our table; nor did I ever hear the slightest suggestion that we should do otherwise.

Winston Churchill,
on the decision at Potsdam in July of 1945 to use the American atomic weapon on Japan

VICTORY!

At 7:00 in the evening on August 14, 1945, President Harry Truman read a statement to a group of reporters gathered at the White House. "I have received this afternoon a message from the Japanese government in reply to the message forwarded to that government by the secretary of state on August 11," Truman announced. "I deem this reply a full acceptance of the Potsdam Declaration which specifies the unconditional surrender of Japan." World War II was finally over. Across America, across the world, people rejoiced. Much work remained to be done; some wounds would heal quickly; others would remain always as reminders of the horrors of warfare. For almost every American, life was different in 1945 than it had been in 1941. The world itself had changed. But on August 14, 1945, what mattered most was that freedom had prevailed and the world was at peace once more.

THE WHITE HOUSE, WASHINGTON, D.C.—President Harry S Truman announces the unconditional surrender of Japan, August 14, 1945. *Photo National Park Service, Courtesy National Archives.*

ON THE USS *MISSOURI* IN TOKYO BAY—General Douglas MacArthur, as supreme Allied commander, signs the official document accepting the unconditional surrender of Japan during formal surrender ceremonies on September 2, 1945. Standing directly behind MacArthur is Lieutenant General Jonathan Wainwright, and to his left is Lieutenant General A. E. Percival, both recently released prisoners of the Japanese. *Photo U.S. Navy, Courtesy National Archives.*

We are gathered here, representatives of the major warring powers, to conclude a solemn agreement whereby peace may be restored. The issues, involving divergent ideals and ideologies, have been determined on the battlefields of the world and hence are not for our discussion or debate. Nor is it for us here to meet, representing as we do a majority of the people of the earth, in a spirit of distrust, malice, or hatred. But rather it is for us, both victors and vanquished, to serve, committing all peoples unreservedly to faithful compliance with the understandings they are here formally to assume. It is my earnest hope ... that from this solemn occasion a better world shall emerge
.... a world dedicated to the dignity of man.... Let us pray that peace be restored to the world, and that God will preserve it always. These proceedings are now closed.

General Douglas MacArthur
September 2, 1945
Tokyo Bay, Japan

ON THE USS *MISSOURI* IN TOKYO BAY—Spectators and photographers line the deck of the USS *Missouri* to watch the formal surrender ceremonies. *Photo U.S. Navy, Courtesy National Archives.*

On May 8, 1945—V-E Day—the war with Germany came to an end. Although we were grateful and relieved that the Allied victory in Europe put an end to unimaginable suffering for so many people, we had to hold our breath for three more months before total victory could be declared; only then would peace prevail throughout the world. Japan's surrender on August 14, 1945, brought the true end of the war and with it an unbelievable feeling of euphoria.

When word of the surrender was broadcast on the radio, people, as if on cue, poured out of their houses onto the streets of cities and towns all over the country. In my hometown of Chelsea, Massachusetts, just north of Boston, friends and neighbors greeted each other with tears and laughter and, in parade-like formation, linked arms and walked to the town square, where they joined others, friends and strangers alike, to march up and down Broadway, kissing and hugging and back-slapping, releasing all the emotion that had been in check for so long.

Sailors and nurses from the nearby naval hospital rushed to join the townspeople. We welcomed them with heartfelt gratitude and warm embraces to show our appreciation for the brave sacrifices of all those who risked their lives to restore peace in the world—both those who made it back home and those who lay in green fields under white crosses in faraway places. As the day came to an end, we slowly made our way home with warm and happy hearts that were tinged with sadness. We remembered the lives lost, soldier and civilian, all over the world; and we offered a prayer of thanks for all those who helped preserve the freedom of the world.

Mary Theodore

TIMES SQUARE, NEW YORK CITY, NEW YORK—In perhaps the most well-known photo of the day, a sailor celebrates victory with a kiss. *Photo Courtesy National Archives.*

NEW YORK CITY, NEW YORK—An Italian-American neighborhood in New York City celebrates the end of the war. *Photo Courtesy National Archives.*

TIMES SQUARE, NEW YORK CITY, NEW YORK—On August 15, 1945, people rush into the street from everywhere to celebrate, to laugh, to cry, and to give thanks that the long nightmare is over. *Photo Courtesy National Archives.*

OVERLEAF: PEARL HARBOR, HAWAII—The USS *Arizona* Memorial, built directly over the sunken *Arizona*— the final resting place for over 1,000 sailors. *Photo T. DelAmo/H. Armstrong Roberts.*

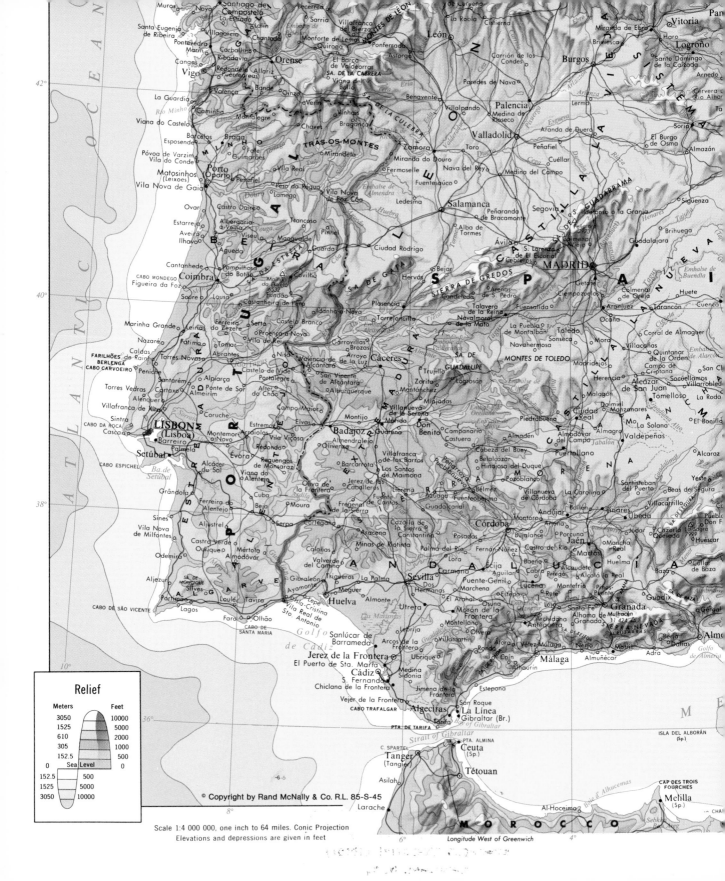

Enchantment of the World

PORTUGAL

By Esther and Wilbur Cross

Consultant: Douglas L. Wheeler, Ph.D., Professor of Modern History, University of New Hampshire, Durham, New Hampshire

Consultant for Reading: Robert L. Hillerich, Ph.D., Bowling Green State University, Bowling Green, Ohio

 CHILDRENS PRESS, CHICAGO

A produce market in Funchal,
capital of the Madeira Islands

Library of Congress Cataloging-in-Publication Data

Cross, Esther,
 Portugal.

 (Enchantment of the world)
 Summary: An introduction to the geography, history,
economy, culture, and people of the country described
as "an island in Europe."
 1. Portugal—Juvenile literature. [1. Portugal]
I. Cross, Wilbur. II. Title. III. Series.
DP517.C76 1986 946.9 85-26991
ISBN 0-516-02778-6

Picture Acknowledgements
© **Joseph A. DiChello, Jr.**—11, 15 (left), 16, 51 (bottom
 right), 58 (right), 74, 75 (2 photos), 83, 86, 93 (right)
© **Robert Frerck/Odyssey Productions, Chicago**—12, 18,
 22, 28, 30, 46, 48 (left), 50 (bottom), 51 (top), 52, 55
 (2 photos), 59, 61, 62 (left), 68, 69, 70 (bottom), 79, 80, 92
 (2 photos), 102 (left), 108, 109
Gartman Agency: © **Michael Philip Manheim**—25 (left)
Hillstrom Stock Photo:
 © **John Apolinski**—101 (right), 105 (left), 106
 (2 photos)
 © **P. Bastin/Explorer**—34
 © **Mary Ann Brockman**—104
 © **Steve Carr**—10, 33 (left), 62 (right), 63, 77 (left), 98
 (top left), 101 (left), 103, 111
 © **Louis Yves Loirat/Explorer**—66
 © **Jack Lund**—17, 64
 © **M. Moisnard/Explorer**—26
 © **Roy/Explorer**—19, 20, 94, 102 (right), 107 (left)
 © **Letty Stasko/Variations in Photography, Inc.**—49
 (right), 82 (right)
 © **William Stenseth/Variations in Photography, Inc.**—5,
 65
 © **H. Vola/Explorer**—67
Historical Pictures Service, Chicago—33 (right), 35, 36,
 37, 41, 89
Image Finders: © **Bob Skelly**—49 (left)
Journalism Services: © **Wolfgang Timmermann**—77
 (right)
Nawrocki Stock Photo: © **Rui Coutinho**—48 (right), 70
 (top), 81 (2 photos), 95, 98 (top right), 105 (right), 110
Chip and Rosa Peterson: © **Stuart Schwartz**—38 (right)
Roloc Color Slides—Cover, 50 (top), 51 (bottom left), 53,
 54 (2 photos), 57 (right), 58 (left), 78, 93 (left)
Root Resources:
 © **Leonard Gordon**—57 (left)
 © **Irene Hubble**—23
 © **Grace H. Lanctot**—82 (left), 98 (bottom left), 107
 (right)
© **M. B. Rosalsky**—38 (left)
© **Daniel A. Rothermel**—98 (bottom right)
© **Bob and Ira Spring**—21, 84
Tom Stack and Associates:
 © **Mickey Gibson**—9
 © **Gary Milburn**—31
 © **Todd Powell**—6
United Press International—40, 42, 43, 44, 45 (2 photos)
Valan Photos:
 © **Pam Hickman**—15 (right), 73, 97
 © **T. Joyce**—4, 25 (right)
Len Meents: Maps on pages 19, 22, 53, 57, 61, 64, 66
Courtesy Flag Research Center, Winchester, MA 01890:
 Flag on back cover
Cover: Sintra Palace and surrounding buildings

*The Douro River
flowing past Oporto*

TABLE OF CONTENTS

Albufeira is both a fishing town and a holiday resort.

Chapter 1

PORTUGAL: THE GENTLE LAND

Portugal has been described as "an island in Europe," part of the continent, yet apart from it; next to Spain, yet distinct from it; a nation that has new outlooks, yet retains the finest of Old World traditions. Its hardy coastlines—to the north, the west, and the south—jut boldly out into the Atlantic Ocean, profiling the country as one that has long been committed to the sea. Indeed, Portugal once was the maritime "stepping stone" from Europe to the New World—to North America, South America, and the Caribbean, as well as to the far reaches of Africa, Australia, and the Far East.

From earliest times, Portugal was a nation of seafarers and explorers. These men opened sea routes during the fifteenth and sixteenth centuries and established a reputation for daring exploits and skillful navigation. When most other European nations were still developing within their own borders, Portugal was importing spices from the East Indies and Ceylon, silver from Japan, and pearls from Persia. Its adventurous navigators were not only enriching the kingdom's trade but were establishing new nations, notably Brazil, Angola, and Portuguese Guinea.

For all of its bold exploits, battles with powerful forces of nature, and stubborn resistance to enemies, Portugal has remained a land that can best be described as "gentle." Its people range from valiant fishermen to farsighted educators, affable politicians, dedicated physicians, and well-to-do merchants. They have a graciousness that endears them to strangers. The comfortable climate along the popular central coast avoids extremities of heat and cold. The mountains, plains, and valleys are contoured with a combination of beauty and utility.

One writer described Portugal as comfortable and unpretentious, "without chic in the French sense or splendor in the British way, but with a certain rough dignity all its own." Yet, as he pointed out, more than two-thirds of our earth was discovered in just one century by skilled Portuguese navigators who ventured across oceans that other nations feared to explore. Such dramatic contrast is evident in much that Portugal has to offer today — a combination of the modest and simple with a grandeur and creative spirit that exists nowhere else in the world.

Portugal is a small nation by European standards, and even smaller by comparison with other major nations of the world. That is one reason why its historical accomplishments are so impressive. One historian has called the Portuguese "the creators of the modern world." Another has likened the early Portuguese navigators to present-day astronauts. Whatever the comparisons, it is clear that the Portuguese leaders in the fifteenth and sixteenth centuries gained a wider knowledge of distant continents and diverse cultures and civilizations than any other European rulers.

Despite the broad outlook that shaped its remarkable history, Portugal is today considered a "developing" country. The reason? Social and economic conditions lag behind those of many major

Mural of one of several Communist parties on a Lisbon street

Western nations. Also, Portugal is still struggling with political turmoil, despite continuing attempts to establish a democratic government. The people themselves, though faced with financial hardships and poor social conditions, continue to be sympathetic and considerate to friends and strangers alike. Their attitude and nature reflect an internal strength that is immediately apparent to foreigners.

Of all the nations of the world, Portugal best retains what could be called a Victorian charm. Visitors who return from Portugal refer to the country as being "Old World" or "like a nineteenth-century painting." They describe the homes and public buildings as gracious, the landscape as soft and muted, the streets as picturesque, the colors as being worthy of watercolors and pastels.

But many visitors, casual and eager to avoid conflicts, do not see the *inner* Portugal as it exists today in the real world. The Portuguese keep their problems to themselves. Poverty is rampant, in the cities, on the farms, even in the once-thriving

Women of Santiago do Cacém whitewashing a fence

world of the navigator and the fisherman. Yet, visitors see few slums like the miserable favelas of South America or the slum areas of large metropolises. The very poorest people keep their sidewalks and rural plots and structures as tidy and spotless as the kitchens of palaces. The only litter ever encountered is in picnic, beach, and parking areas frequented by tourists, a rather shameful commentary on the carelessness of outsiders.

"To be poor in Portugal," wrote a noted sociologist, "is much less disagreeable than to be poor in the outworn industrial communities of northern Europe." The people are supportive of one another, sharing whatever they have and making sure that no one suffers. Money goes farther in Portugal, and is more respected, than in almost any other Western nation. There are almost no public beggars and very few street sellers trying to unload shoddy merchandise on unwary tourists. Most of the street selling is done by families who operate stands or carts and proudly offer their handmade goods.

Typical oxcart transportation

For the most part, the Portuguese are perceptive. They recognize the country's past glory and realize that the realities of modern life have eroded much of that ancient majesty. They do not, however, attempt to explain away their economic and social plight. They accept it with philosophic grace, even humor, taking the attitude that the future will be brighter and some of the old glories regained. In contrast to the outlook of some of the poverty-stricken Latin nations, however, this is not a matter of putting things off—*manhã, manhã,* ''tomorrow, tomorrow.'' The fishermen spend long hours at sea; the farmers go early to the fields; the merchants tend carefully to their shops; the professional people bring diligence and care to their callings.

Portugal is, to outsiders, one of the least familiar nations of Europe. Yet it is also one of the most fascinating of countries to study because it has so many appealing facets—and so many enigmas.

Much of the Douro River valley is terraced for farming.

Chapter 2

A NATION IN MINIATURE

Although Portugal is popularly known today as an "island" in Europe because it differs in so many ways from its neighbors, it is anything but an island geographically. In shape, it is long and narrow, lying on the western edge of the Iberian Peninsula. It is bordered by Spain to the north and east and by the Atlantic Ocean to the west and south. The country is divided into three distinct regions by the two principal rivers, the Douro and the Tagus. The Douro flows from east to west, entering the Atlantic at Oporto, one of the major seaports. The Tagus flows in a more southwesterly direction, broadening into a wide bay at Lisbon, the nation's capital and principal city.

To some extent there are climatic differences in these three regions, ranging from the cooler northern lands to the sunny Algarve in the south. But since Portugal is only about 350 miles (563 kilometers) long from north to south, there is little change. The climate is mild and generally comfortable all year, except in

the northern and central mountains, where temperature and climate can vary considerably. The highest range is Serra da Estrela, located between the two main rivers and forming a ridge that rises to 6,545 feet (1,995 meters). This ridge subdivides the central section from north to south, so that it divides the coastal plain on the west from the Iberian plateau on the east.

South of the Tagus River lies the flat plain of the Alentejo, sometimes referred to as the "granary of Portugal," though the soil is not rich and requires constant irrigation. This area is, in turn, separated from the southern coastal plain of the Algarve by a range of hills, mostly low and rolling and with none over 1,800 feet (549 meters). The Algarve coast, with its series of beaches and rocky promontories, resembles the northern shores of Morocco, which lies just to the south, at the entrance to the Mediterranean. Indeed, the Algarve was inhabited at one time by the Moors and still shows evidence of the Moorish influence.

Portugal, covering some 34,000 square miles (89,000 square kilometers), is about the same size as Indiana or Hungary. Although there are many natural, open plains, one-third of the country is still heavily wooded. There are rich forests of pine, oak, and eucalyptus, many of them planted during recent reforestation projects. But many go back centuries to the days when Portuguese kings enacted laws that protected the forests from the axes of farmers and shipbuilders. Cork trees are also abundant, for Portugal supplies more than half of the world's cork. These trees are protected by strict regulations so that the bark is stripped without damaging the tree.

Many people tend to speak of Portugal and Spain in the same breath, but the faces of the two nations are completely different. Portugal has a greater variety of landscapes that are readily

Mountain forests near Manteigas (left) and wildflowers in the northern mountains (right)

apparent, even in short drives of an hour or so. Portugal has been called "the wild garden of Europe" because of the richness of its natural growth, ranging from widely differing species of wildflowers to varying stands and groves of trees. Altitude, rainfall, or soil composition can change quickly within a radius of 100 miles (161 kilometers) or so.

Very little has been written about the wildflowers of Portugal, though they compare favorably with Alpine flowers. The uplands of the southern region, for example, are carpeted with quiltlike patterns of scarlet and gold, purple and white, blue and yellow. There are chrysanthemums and poppies, bluebells and iris, narcissus and daffodils, and stark white moondaisies. These flowers, along with sweeps of heather and clumps of cacti and strangely twisted vines, color the map of Portugal in the plains and plateaus and along the rivers and byways.

Clouds and mists shroud the Serra da Estrela mountains.

The mountains—as rugged and dramatic as they may be—are often carpeted with bushes, vines, mosses, and upland plants so that their contours are soft and lush. Nourished by rains and frequent mists, the land looks somewhat like the lake districts of England or Ireland, padded with foliage in a variety of greens and browns and occasional swatches of pastels. In the south, the mountains and hills tend to be much drier and more barren. There, the predominant colors are the earth hues, with outcroppings of yellow or bronze or rust.

Then there is the sea—the "theme" that binds the country together, historically, economically, sociologically, and culturally. From any point in Portugal, the sea is never far away. Even the widest sections of the country are barely 125 miles (201 kilometers) across. Large rivers like the Douro, the Tagus, and the Mondego form broad bays and estuaries where they flow into the

The Serra de Sintra range ends in the Cabo da Roca, a sheer cliff over the sea.

Atlantic. Thus, the salty seawater washes twenty-five to thirty miles (forty to forty-eight kilometers) upstream, so that people who live that far inland feel closely allied to the sea.

One popular guide to Portugal referred to the country as a "Gateway to the Oceans"—a kind of huge breakwater against which waves and currents dashed and ocean storms blew themselves out. Half of the country's entire border lies on the sea—more than five hundred miles (eight hundred kilometers) of coastline that is in itself geologically unique. Along the maritime borders of this small nation, you can find just about every form of oceanfront terrain that exists in temperate zones. In some sections, whole mountains plunge from heights of two to three thousand feet (six to nine hundred meters) right into the sea, just as they do in the fjords of Norway. Other sections are composed of steep cliffs reminiscent of the Amalfi Coast of Italy. Strange volcanic

Rock formations at Praia da Rocha on the Algarve coast

formations and sea-sculptured rocks abound along the southern coast, resembling Hawaiian lava flows that have been cooled, eroded, and chiseled by the action of wind and waves.

Bays and estuaries, inlets and gulfs, coves and lagoons come in an astonishing array of sizes and forms, some completely natural and others shaped by the hand of man. Portugal is noted, too, for its beaches. Many are small and private, protected by jutting fingers of rock. Others are long and narrow, or long and broad, or a combination of smooth sand and gentle dunes. They range in consistency from jelly-bean-sized pebbles to sugar-grained sand, and in color from almost black to tones of browns and grays and beiges to pure white.

Peneda Gerês National Park and Lake Salamonda in the northern Minho region

THE THREE REGIONS

The variety of Portugal's natural features is so unusual that it is almost necessary to look at each region separately.

The northern region consists of the Trás-os-Montes and Minho areas, which are made up to a great extent by the southern extension of the Galician ranges of Spain. The land is rugged and the climate generally temperate, with abundant pine and chestnut forests covering the mountainsides.

Many people have likened the north to Scotland, not only because of its physical characteristics but also because of the humidity and the mists that shroud the mountains.

Torre Peak, the highest point in the Serra da Estrela range

This region is considered the "birthplace" of Portugal. Its very ruggedness may account for the nature of those early Portuguese who were so devoted to exploration in the far corners of the globe.

The central region, known as the land between the two great rivers, is in sharp contrast. It consists mainly of a highland area in the east, along the Spanish border, that slopes down to a coastal plain in the west. This plain is called alluvial because it is composed largely of alluvium—sand, silt, clay, and gravel deposited by rivers, streams, and rainfall. The highland area includes the Serra da Estrela, with many sections of remote wilderness and deep forests. Snowfall is common here in winter, lasting from late autumn until early spring. The central region also includes the largest city in Portugal, Lisbon, and the great academic center, Coimbra.

The central region has probably the greatest extremes of

Cornfield in the central plains

temperature, ranging from the winter cold in the mountains to the summer heat of the lowlands. Where it is not cold enough for snow, rain and fog are commonplace in the winter.

The Tagus River forms a sharp dividing line. To its south lie wide, flat plains, largely cultivated in grains such as corn, wheat, and, in some sectors, rice. The land is patterned, not with small farms, but with large agricultural estates. The streams are generally small and susceptible to drought, so that irrigation is necessary during the drier months. The lack of rain, so worrisome to the farmers of the plains, is an asset to those who live farther south in the Algarve. It is here that the Portuguese and many tourists from Europe and America come during the late spring and summer to soak up the sun and enjoy the beaches. Many foreigners, too, have now taken up permanent residences in the Algarve. They do not care to see rain or mists.

Cape St. Vincent

Geographically, this southern coast is more closely related to Morocco than to central and northern Portugal. Its physical features and summer climate are like those on the North African coast. Its architecture and way of life show the Moorish influence.

The western extremity of the Algarve, known as Cape St. Vincent, is the southwestern tip of continental Europe. It was once believed that Portugal's sea captains received their information here from the famous Henry the Navigator before setting sail on voyages of discovery. Recent historians have disproved this; nevertheless, the landscape is appropriate for tales of adventure: remote, rockbound, treacherous to strangers, and always fuming with surf and spray from the relentless pounding of the Atlantic.

THE MADEIRAS

Madeira was visited by Portuguese navigators in 1419 and over the years has become one of Portugal's most treasured possessions

Harbor on Madeira's principal island

because of its physical beauty, its delightful climate, and its location. The Madeira archipelago—a group of islands—is situated in the North Atlantic some 400 miles (644 kilometers) west of Morocco and about 650 miles (1,046 kilometers) southwest of Lisbon. It consists of the main island of Madeira, the small island of Porto Santo, and two groups of uninhabited islands, the Desertas and the Selvagens.

Madeira was formed by a submerged volcano that erupted from the sea millions of years ago. Long and narrow in shape, the entire island is really a huge mountaintop. Its purple-green peaks drop sharply into deep valleys in the interior. Along the island's perimeter, the peaks shear off as precipitous cliffs of dark volcanic rock known as basalt. Dense tropical foliage covers most of the island. The early Romans, who first discovered the group, referred to them as the Purple Islands. The Portuguese selected the name Madeira, which means "wood," because of the dense forests covering the main island.

Although Madeira is barely 35 miles (56 kilometers) long, its rugged mountains rise more than 6,000 feet (1,829 meters). Their beauty is enhanced by the corrugated pattern of the ridges and valleys that slope down to the sea. The Madeirans use these ridges as natural channels to carry irrigation water to their ample plantings of bananas, grapes, sugarcane, barley, and sweet potatoes. There is hardly a square foot of the rich volcanic soil that has not been cultivated. The visual effect from the air is that of a huge patchwork quilt draped over an irregular mound in the middle of the ocean.

The towns have also taken full advantage of the climate and rich soil. The avenues and narrow byways are resplendent with flowers and blossoming trees. These include laburnum and jacaranda, lilies and mimosa, orchids and roses. In some places, brilliant bougainvillea vines are so thick on their arbors that they resemble big red tents. Formal gardens are lush with exotic plants from all over the world. They include species from Australia, China, Japan, the Pacific islands, South America, Malaya, and Madagascar.

On the lower, southern slopes of the mountains lies Madeira's capital and largest city, Funchal. Its steep streets rise up the slopes and intersect hundreds of encircling terraces. These terraces have been built and maintained over many years to hold the soil and moisture in place. From afar, they look like ripples in the steep hillsides, patterns of lush green surrounded by white buildings and red tile roofs.

Quaint modes of transportation were devised early in Madeira's history to cope with the steep streets. A few of these are still used in some sections of Funchal. They include ox carts, palanquins (chairlike contraptions attached to poles and carried by two men),

Wicker sled in Funchal (left). Terraced Madeiran land and irrigation canal (right)

hammocks slung on the shoulders, and a kind of large sled that slides down slippery, black-pebbled lanes. The sleds—famous tourist attractions—take many a visitor careening down the narrow streets, skillfully guided by young men wearing straw hats and baggy trousers.

Like mainland Portugal, Madeira is wedded to the sea. Protective forts and lighthouses ring the coast. Its ports are active with sailboats and other pleasure craft. Fishermen range far out to sea in search of tuna, scabbard fish, swordfish, and shellfish, many of which are exported. Yet, unlike the Algarve or the coastal resort areas west of Lisbon, Madeira has very few soft, sandy beaches. Much of the coastline is composed of cliffs that plunge straight down into the ocean.

Sete Cidades crater lake on São Miguel island in the Azores

THE AZORES

Portugal's other important islands are the Azores. These nine islands are strung across the Atlantic Ocean, with the easternmost islands lying 870 miles (1,400 kilometers) west of Lisbon. Like Madeira, they are submarine peaks that rose from depths of 10,000 feet (3,048 meters) or more during intense volcanic action millions of years ago. Today they are covered with thick, green vegetation, made all the more lush by rainfall and mists.

The principal islands are São Miguel, Santa Maria, and Terceira. Ponta Delgada, the capital of the Azores, is located on São Miguel, the largest of the islands, which has several interesting geological features. One of these is Sete Cidades crater, where bright blue lakes can be seen shimmering far below. Another is Furnas Valley, where there are steep precipices, a turquoise lake, and a cluster of boiling sulfur springs.

The nine islands, all of which are volcanic and mountainous, with peaks rising as high as 7,600 feet (2,316 meters), are not always calm. They are subject to eruptions and earthquakes, hurricanes, and other fierce North Atlantic storms. They can also lie shrouded in fog and mists for long periods of time.

Despite the fickleness of the weather, the islands have luxuriant vegetation that stems from both Europe and Africa. Crops include oranges and other citrus fruits, pineapples, grapes, tea, grains, tobacco, and all kinds of vegetables. The Azores are also dependent upon the sea. The harbors are filled with craft ranging from small boats to ocean liners. Fishing is an active industry, and at one time the Azores were an important whaling center.

Lying across a 390-mile (628-kilometer) stretch of the Atlantic the Azores have served continents on both sides of the ocean as a transportation and communications center. The western tip of the archipelago lies only 2,300 miles (3,700 kilometers) from New York City.

On Christopher Columbus's voyage back from the West Indies in 1493, he made his first stop on Santa Maria island. Santa Maria's airport is now a major landing strip for several international commercial airlines. Vasco da Gama landed on the island of Terceira on his return voyage from India in 1499. The North Atlantic Treaty Organization (NATO) has had its major Atlantic military air base there since World War II. The island of Horta was the landing point in 1919 for the first airplane to cross the Atlantic. Horta is now the center for transatlantic cables and an important radio communication center.

Although the transportation and communication industries provide employment to many Azoreans, there is heavy emigration from the Azores to the United States and other countries.

Citania de Briteiros, Portugal's oldest known settlement, existed from the 800s B.C. to the 400s B.C. Its walls enclosed 150 huts.

Chapter 3
OLD WORLD EUROPE
IN A NUTSHELL

Sometime after the year 1000 B.C., a group of tribes known as the Celts swept across the European continent, eventually crossing into the British Isles. Mounted on swift horses, armed with iron weapons, and speaking loose Indo-European dialects, they managed to subdue many of the peoples who opposed them. Having established colonies over a wide region, they dominated the land largely because of their knowledge of mining and their ability to make weapons and utensils of iron. Thus, they thrived in what has become known as the Iron Age of central Europe.

One group of Celts settled in the Iberian Peninsula, the territory now occupied by Portugal and Spain. The western edge of the peninsula was known as Lusitania to the ancient Romans, who eyed the region as a rich land ripe for conquest.

The Roman ruins at Conimbriga, near Coimbra. During the Iron Age, long before the Romans arrived, a Celtic city stood here.

Around 200 B.C., the Romans started voyages of conquest, intent on bringing Lusitania into the spreading Roman Empire. But they faced heavy resistance by the Lusitanians, who were led by Viriatus, a popular warrior and chief. His army defeated the Roman troops decisively in 147 B.C., and repulsed all attacks for the next eight years. But then the Romans, promising lasting peace and prosperity, bribed Viriatus's own emissaries to assassinate him. This made it possible for Rome to annex all of Lusitania.

The Romans, under Julius Caesar, Augustus, and other rulers, colonized Lusitania and built towns and forts, the ruins of which may still be seen today. Among the most extensive Roman ruins are those at Conimbriga, which lies about 110 miles (177 kilometers) north of Lisbon, near the city of Coimbra.

The new colony of Lusitania thrived for a time, adopting Roman ways and language. It was from the Latin of the Romans that the Portuguese language was derived.

Battlement walls of the Moors' Castle in Sintra

END OF THE ROMAN ERA

At the beginning of the fifth century A.D., Roman rule was threatened when the Visigoths began to invade parts of the Iberian Peninsula. These invaders were people of German origin who had gradually, sometimes peacefully, spread westward across Europe into France and Spain. By the time some of them had reached Portugal they were strong enough to drive the Romans out and develop their own settlements. The Visigoths remained in many regions of Portugal for some two hundred years. Then they, in turn, were threatened by a new wave of invaders.

The Moors, nomadic peoples from the northern coast of Africa, began to take over much of the Iberian Peninsula after defeating the Visigoths in 711. In Portugal they settled mainly along the Algarve coast. The Moors retained their foothold in the Iberian Peninsula from the eighth to the tenth century.

The origins of Portugal as an independent nation can be traced to the eleventh century, when the king of Spain called Henry of Burgundy and other French noblemen to assist in driving out the Moors. For Henry's part in the battles, he was given a portion of land in Coimbra, Portugal, and the title count of Coimbra. Later this title was changed to king of Portugal.

When Henry died, he left his land to his son Afonso Henriques, who soon pronounced himself Afonso I, king of Portugal. When Afonso won a victory over the Moors in his territory in 1139, the Spanish monarchy was convinced that he was fit to rule. Spain recognized Portugal's independence in 1143.

About three-fourths of the present area of Portugal was now under Afonso I. But he was unable to push the Moors out of the southern part of the country. His problems were multiplied because of continual strife with the Catholic church over lands and power, the need to rebuff claimants to his throne, and the cost of rebuilding towns damaged in battle.

Afonso I was followed by King Sancho I, who reigned from 1185 until 1211; Afonso II, from 1211 until 1223; and Sancho II, from 1223 until 1248. All of these rulers failed in persistent attempts to drive the Moors from southern Portugal. Finally, in 1249, Afonso III was able to muster forces strong enough to drive the rest of the Moors from the Algarve, along the southern coast. Portugal was finally consolidated from border to border, a monarchy free from invasion or domination.

THE GOLDEN ERA OF DISCOVERY

Very little of consequence happened in Portugal during the next hundred years. In that period the new nation was trying to

Left: Statue of Afonso Henriques, first king of Portugal, in Lisbon
Right: Prince Henry the Navigator

resolve internal disputes and settle differences with Spain and other countries. But the nation was gradually becoming stronger. By the end of the fourteenth century, the Portuguese under King João I were strong enough to defeat an army of Castilians in the Battle of Aljubarrota. This victory firmly established the authority of King João of the House of Aviz, after a bitter struggle over the succession to the throne. King João and his queen, Philippa, ushered in the most glorious era in Portugal's history.

One of the sons of João and Philippa was Prince Henry, known to history as Henry the Navigator. A man of great skill and vision, he encouraged Portuguese ship captains to set forth on innumerable voyages of exploration and discovery. One of his captains was Vasco da Gama, who discovered the route to India and made it possible for Portugal to earn great riches through the development of the spice trade.

The caravels revolutionized navigation. Their triangular sails could pivot around the mast, so the ships could reach great speeds and sail very close to oncoming winds.

Henry himself spent little time at sea. Rather, he gathered together the finest sea captains, chart makers, astronomers, and navigators he could find. Together, they prepared new charts of the oceans and seas and developed new principles of navigation. They also created a new type of ship, the caravel, which was the first ship that could be sailed in a direction other than before the wind. The caravel made it possible for sea captains to plan their courses without being at the mercy of the wind's direction.

Henry the Navigator made it possible for Portuguese navigators to undertake long-range voyages of exploration such as they had never attempted before. They soon discovered Madeira and the Azores, and were easily able to reach the coasts of North Africa. Gradually they explored south along the African coast. In 1488, an

Vasco da Gama negotiating a trade agreement with an Indian ruler

exciting discovery was made when one of the most famous navigators, Bartolomeu Dias, reached the Cape of Good Hope at the southern tip of Africa. It was nine years later that Vasco da Gama embarked on the famous two-year voyage that took him from Lisbon, around Africa, and to India.

Finding sea routes to Asia meant that trading in spices, silks, and precious stones and metals could be done more quickly and more safely. Overland transportation, by caravan, required travel through hostile lands, where the caravans were easily attacked and robbed and their traders murdered.

In 1495, one of Portugal's most notable monarchs ascended to the throne. He was Manuel I, called "Manuel the Fortunate" because of the wealth and influence of his times. Lisbon was

Manuel I "The Fortunate"

developing into the richest and most beautiful city in Europe. Portugal was powerful enough to "divide the world in two," sharing with Spain an astonishing pact that literally defined the entire globe as two hemispheres—one that could be explored by Portugal and the other by Spain. No other nation could dispute this treaty at the end of the fifteenth century, for none possessed the ships and navigators capable of ranging the far seas.

During the rule of Manuel, Portuguese exploration and discoveries reached their height. One of the first great seagoing achievements was the discovery of Brazil by Pedro Álvares Cabral in 1500. Eleven years later another famous Portuguese navigator, Ferdinand Magellan, began exploring the Spice Islands and made further discoveries in India. Magellan's most famous voyage lasted from 1519 to 1521. It was then that he located the strait that bears his name, at the tip of South America, and became the first sea captain whose ship circumnavigated the globe.

King Sebastião meets his death in the ill-fated battle of Alcazarquivir in Morocco. Since he was a boy, Sebastião had dreamed of leading a crusade against the Moors.

DECLINE AND RESTORATION

When the last member of the once-powerful House of Aviz died, Portugal was a nation in turmoil. Its army had been committed to a fatal crusade in Morocco in 1578, during which the king was killed, along with thousands of his best soldiers. Philip II of Spain seized this tragic opportunity to assume the crown of Portugal as well as his own, and was able to do so with very little resistance. For sixty years Portugal remained in what was grimly referred to as "Spanish captivity." Not only did the country forfeit precious independence, but it was stripped of many of its overseas territories. The Spanish monarchy, more interested in exploiting Portugal and usurping its riches, did little to develop the commerce and trade that navigators had established during the fifteenth and sixteenth centuries.

Left: Two houses in Lisbon's Alfama district that collapsed against each other in the earthquake of 1755. Right: King João VI

Led by a group of noblemen who had everything to gain and little to lose, the Portuguese people finally revolted and reestablished independence. The noblemen selected their most powerful cohort, the Duke of Braganca, to take over Portugal's long-vacant throne. As João IV, crowned in 1640, he resisted further Spanish invasions, but only by resorting to constant and costly battles to protect his borders. He himself depleted the treasury by erecting many lavish buildings at a time when the country was barely able to keep the people from starvation.

During the reign of King José I, from 1750 to 1777, two factors helped to sustain the economy of Portugal. One was the appointment of the Marquis of Pombal as premiere. Pombal, though criticized by many noblemen for being too dictatorial, used his office to promote the economic progress of the country. He was said to have more power than the king himself. When Lisbon was devastated by a great earthquake in 1755, it was he who took charge and began rebuilding the city.

The second factor, sometimes referred to as the nation's "saving grace," was Brazil. During this period, motivated by Pombal's efforts to increase trade, Portugal's large South American colony supplied precious gems, gold, fine lumber, and other goods.

Pombal might have accomplished a great deal more during his term as premiere. But he was expelled from office after the death of José I, largely because he was considered to be a despot who had little consideration for the rights of others. However, he left behind certain reforms, as well as important public structures. He had fostered agricultural development, built roads, improved communications, and constructed several new towns.

During the reign that followed, under Maria I and her husband, Peter III, the fortunes of Portugal again declined. By the beginning of the nineteenth century, an alliance with England stirred up the hatred of the French. In 1807, Napoleon's forces invaded Portugal, as well as Spain, touching off what was known as the Peninsular War (because it took place in the Iberian Peninsula). The royal family, including Maria's son who was soon to become King João VI, fled to Brazil.

The French were driven out of Portugal in 1811, but it was several years before João VI reestablished his royal family in Lisbon. In the meantime, Portugal's style of government had changed from an absolute monarchy to a constitutional monarchy and Brazil had declared independence, with Pedro I (João's elder son) as emperor.

From about this time on, the monarchy fell gradually into disfavor among the people, largely because of a lack of leadership, family squabbles, and numerous internal plots. Certain groups of moderates and liberals, however, managed to institute some important reforms in the country.

Manuel II, exiled king of Portugal, with Queen Augusta, enjoying a tennis tournament in Cannes, France

END OF THE MONARCHY

The end came with a sudden, tragic shock. After many changes in rulership, Carlos I came to the throne in 1889. His powers were greatly limited. The country was, in fact, governed largely by various parties and finally, in 1906, by the prime minister, João Franco, who was a kind of conservative dictator.

By 1907, Carlos I was enmeshed in political intrigue, despite his efforts to avoid controversy. Then, on February 1, 1908, as he and his elder son, Luís Filipe, rode in an open carriage across one of the main squares of Lisbon, the end came. They were both assassinated. The younger son, eighteen-year-old Prince Manuel,

Teófilo Braga, a writer and the first president of the Portuguese Republic (fifth from left), with his council of ministers

devastated by the assassination but anxious to avoid plunging Portugal into a civil war, later renounced all rights to the throne and withdrew to England. Thus ended the monarchy, after the first regicide (killing of a king) in Portuguese history.

In 1910, following the abdication of Manuel II, the First Republic was established. With Teófilo Braga as president, this was Portugal's first attempt at democracy. Although the republic lasted sixteen years, the change of government did not solve the country's chronic political and economic problems. Portugal was disrupted by constant rebellions and government takeovers. This brief era saw a succession of forty-five changes of cabinet and nine of the presidency.

A 1941 photo of President Carmona (left) and the powerful prime minister he appointed in 1932, António Salazar

By 1926, the nation was ripe for a dictatorship. There seemed to be no democratic solutions to the problems, since no one party could gather strength or even come to working agreements with other parties. That year, General António Óscar de Fragoso Carmona headed a military coup and easily overthrew the shaky government. Two years later, he was elected president, an office he held until his death in 1951.

Carmona concentrated his initial efforts on trying to strengthen the economy of the country. One of his initial steps was to appoint António de Oliveira Salazar as his minister of finance. Salazar, who had been professor of political economy at the University of Coimbra, brought a considerable amount of order to the economic chaos. As a result of his accomplishments, he was appointed prime minister in 1932.

Salazar (left) in 1959, still prime minister, with President Américo Tomaz

During the Carmona regime the Portuguese currency was stabilized and there was moderate prosperity. Nonetheless, individual and political liberties were restricted, the country was not yet a true democracy. Salazar became increasingly influential. He had a strong hand in all major governmental decisions and was largely responsible for a new constitution that was incorporated in 1933. After that, he really functioned as a dictator, holding enough power to suppress all political opposition.

The Salazar government kept the country neutral during World War II, although it did allow the Allies to construct air bases in the Azores. Consequently, Portugal was not as disrupted by the war as were many smaller nations that had joined the war effort. Despite this stability, Salazar found himself facing more frequent protests from political opponents.

Angolan rebels training for the revolution that drained Portugal's treasury

By 1959, Salazar's power was in decline. It was greatly weakened that year when he pushed through an amendment, very unpopular with the people, stating that the president should be chosen by an electoral college rather than by popular vote. By the 1960s, he was physically ill, suffering a stroke that forced his retirement in 1968. His dictatorship had lasted for four decades.

THE MODERN STATE

Salazar was succeeded by another former professor, Marcello Caetano, who had taught law at the University of Lisbon. Caetano, as prime minister, eased some of the political and individual restrictions. However, he was unable to control the unrest in the colonies. Armed battles with guerrillas in the

Marcello Caetano, Salazar's successor (left), and António de Spínola (right), whose military junta overthrew Caetano's government

African territories became more and more costly. Soon about 40 percent of Portugal's entire budget was being devoted to military spending, draining the country's resources.

By 1974, widespread dissatisfaction with political suppression, the weakening economy, and seemingly endless wars in the colonies came to a head. On April 25 of that year, the government was seized by a military junta, led by General António de Spínola, who was named president. The new government gave independence to a number of the colonies, including Guinea-Bissau, Mozambique, Angola, and the Cape Verde Islands.

The presidency has changed hands several times since, and there has been a degree of continuing political turmoil among the major parties. Unsuccessful with either democracy or dictatorship since 1910, Portugal is still experimenting with democracy.

An overview of Lisbon's tiled roofs and, beyond, the wide mouth of the Tagus

Chapter 4

NEIGHBORING CITIES
AND TOWNS

Portugal has been described as "Europe the Way It Used to Be." Its citizens are polite, considerate, and often quite formal in manner. Many parts of the country still possess the charm of the nineteenth century, along with twentieth-century conveniences. But it is Lisbon, the capital and by far the largest city in Portugal, that sets the tone and pace of the whole country.

LISBON

Lisbon is a city of great dimension—topographically, historically, and culturally. It is a city of seven high hills and innumerable valleys and plateaus. They spread upward from the great Tagus River, which at Lisbon becomes a large bay that blends with the Atlantic Ocean. It is a place of dramatic contrasts—where wide boulevards are joined by narrow, cobblestoned alleyways; where tiny, centuries-old Moorish townhouses lie in the shadows of elegant public buildings; where

Lisbon's "New City" (left) and its old quarter, Alfama (right)

modern commerical towers rise from the clustered, orange-tiled rooftops of modest, two-story apartments; where frantic taxi traffic competes with miniature trolleys.

Lisbon's "old world" lies along the side streets and alleys of ancient quarters where the buildings are close together, often colored in subtle pastels or faced in bright mosaic. The windows and balconies are alive with flowering plants, above which often flap articles of laundry that rival the colors of the blossoms. Up and down these passageways, hawkers balance straw baskets on their heads, filled with huge cabbages, thick-skinned oranges, or bunches of fat strawberries bedded on ferns. Other vendors trail tiny two-wheeled carts with freshly caught flounder, sole, prawns, or clams. Others pass by, balancing huge baskets of flowers or loaves of freshly baked bread, or even wooden cages jammed with live chickens.

St. George's Castle garden is home to white peacocks.

Many of the old quarters of the city are near the Rossio, the main square. The streets in the Baixa, or "Lower Town," are comprised of about a hundred narrow roads, whose short blocks are crowded with stores, commercial houses, and living quarters. Sandwiched in between are tiny shops selling pastries, ice cream, beverages, or ready-to-eat foods. A few merchants even set up tiny curbside tables at which they serve the popular *cafe com leite* (coffee with milk), often with sweets.

There are sections, too, like the Alfama, the old Moorish quarter on the slopes of one of the most famous of Lisbon's hills, crowned by the majestic ruins of the Castle of St. George. The castle, now the main element in a public park that has a magnificent view of the city, was once a Visigoth fort. The Alfama, which was somehow spared during the great earthquake of 1755, is a maze of twisting streets rimmed by clusters of Moorish-style houses.

Lisbon: A flower stand (above) and the monument to the Marquis of Pombal (below)

Above: Lisbon's shipyards. Below: Monument to the Discoveries (left) is a gigantic stylized ship on whose prow stands Henry the Navigator, leading a host of explorers, statesmen, and artists. A view toward Rossio Square (right)

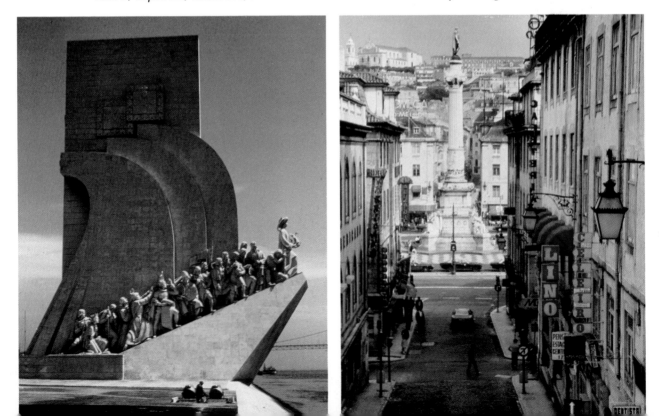

Lisbon's bridge over the Tagus is the longest single-span suspension bridge in Europe. In the background on the left is the towering statue of Cristo Rei (Christ in Majesty).

Beyond the charm and the Old World atmosphere, though, Lisbon is a major European port, with a very deep harbor at the mouth of the Tagus River. Because it is strategically located on the Atlantic Ocean and has one of the best harbors in Europe, Lisbon has long been a hub of shipping and maritime commerce. It is also the cultural and administrative center of the nation, and the prime magnet that draws tourists and other visitors to Portugal from all over the world.

Many of Lisbon's buildings are modern, twentieth-century structures. Its transportation facilities include an international airport, subway, suburban railway lines, and parkways. Among the city's most prominent features is the April 25 Bridge over the Tagus River, one of the longest suspension bridges in the world, beneath a towering statue of Christ.

Estoril's casino attracts an international resort clientele.

THE SUBURBS OF LISBON

To the west of Lisbon, easily reached in less than an hour by car, train, or bus, lies what is popularly known as the "Sun Coast." This is largely a vacation region, though several villages along the coast are still active fishing ports where small boats and trawlers put out to sea from dawn until dusk. Some of the more significant towns are Estoril, Queluz, Cascais, and Sintra.

Estoril is a fashionable seaside resort town with a mild, temperate climate. It offers wide beaches, palm-shaded gardens, luxury hotels, golf and tennis, and other facilities that attract Portuguese vacationers and foreign tourists alike. It was once a popular summer gathering place for members of the royal family and the nobility.

The palace at Queluz (left) once housed Portugal's royalty.
Cascais (right) is both a fishing port and a resort.

Queluz, several miles inland, is the site of a famous eighteenth-century palace that was once the home of the royal family. It is often called the "Portuguese Versailles" because of its elegant interiors and its magnificent gardens, with boxwood hedges, fountains, ponds, and multicolored designs in glazed tiles. Today this is an important attraction for tourists, who come to admire its intricately painted ceilings, crystal chandeliers, and priceless art.

Cascais is an active fishing village that is also a fine vacation resort. Colorful fishing vessels are anchored in its well-protected harbor alongside large yachts and other pleasure craft. The shore is made up of small beaches and rocky cliffs. Many famous people have lived here in the summertime, including royalty from all over Europe.

Just outside the mountain town of Sintra (left) stands Pena Palace (right), on one of the highest peaks in the Serra de Sintra range.

Sintra, a mountain town, is completely different from the communities along the coast. Nestled in the lush, green Serra de Sintra range, the town was once referred to by the English poet Lord Byron as a "glorious Eden." The walled villas, rich gardens, homes, and shops cling to the sides of innumerable hills. They are reached only by narrow, twisting, cobblestone roads that are many centuries old. Crowning a peak is one of the most notable fortresses in Europe, Pena Palace. It was built in the mid-nineteenth century on the site of a sixteenth-century monastery. Because of its origins and additions, it mixes Moorish, Gothic, Renaissance, and baroque styles. Much of it is considered "Manueline," a style of architecture dating back to the time of Manuel I, who promoted Portugal's glorious culture in the fifteenth century.

COSTA DE PRATA

The Costa de Prata region of Portugal hugs the western coast north of the Sun Coast. Its towns are small and seemingly insignificant when compared with the major communities near Lisbon. Yet the region is representative of the country and provides a kind of microscopic view of community life as it is today—and as it has been for many generations.

Coimbra, the largest town in the region, has a population of some 71,000 people. A center of culture and education, it has the second oldest university in the world, the University of Coimbra, founded in the year 1290. Coimbra was the capital of the country under the first king of Portugal in the sixteenth century. The town is built in tiers on a promontory of the Mondego River, some twenty miles from the Atlantic. Many of its streets are as ancient as its origins, closely packed with residences and shops, and dominated by the tall square tower of the university. One street is so crooked, steep, and narrow that it has jokingly been nicknamed *Quebra Costas* (the "broken back").

One of the most unusual attractions in all of Europe is *Portugal dos Pequenitos* ("Portugal of the Little Ones"). This is a spacious garden containing miniature replicas of every type of building in the country and its overseas provinces. There are royal palaces, ancient monasteries, historic monuments, walled villas, public buildings, modest farms, agricultural estates, tropical huts, and many others—all faithfully reproduced to scale.

Obidos, a medieval fortress city, still maintains the high stone walls that protected it from invaders in the twelfth century. Its small, whitewashed homes and shops are bunched together in clusters within the walls, many with tiny balconies full of flowers

Óbidos, with its fortress walls (left). Sardines drying in Nazaré (right)

and plants. Óbidos is rich in history, not only as the fortress home of kings and queens, but as the site where the British troops won their first substantial victory over the French during the Peninsular War. The nearby Lagoon of Óbidos has sheltered boats of every description from ancient times until today, and long ago became known as the source of plentiful supplies of fish and waterfowl.

Nazaré, one of the oldest and most visited fishing villages in all of Portugal, is divided into two parts. One is the crescent-shaped beach section, with its flotilla of brightly decorated fishing boats, which are still built with ancient Phoenician prows that bear the symbols of animals and birds and fish. The other is the upper village, Sitio, which perches on rocky cliffs overlooking the sea. The fishermen's houses ring the sea, forming a colorful border against the rich farmlands that stretch inland toward the soft, rolling hills.

Tomar's Castle of the Templars (left). Harvesting seaweed near Aveiro (right)

Tomar is a village that many Portuguese consider to be the prettiest in the region, if not the country. From its Castle of the Templars, Portuguese knights repulsed the attacks of the Moors in 1190. Just outside the village, Tomar Monastery crowns a verdant hill. It is a broad complex of buildings, with seven main cloisters that range in date from the twelfth to the seventeenth century.

Aveiro, called "the Venice of Portugal," is surrounded by salt flats, beaches, and lagoons. The town is dominated by its Central Canal, from which radiates a system of irrigation canals and protective dikes. It is a strange sight to look toward the town from a low point and see small vessels that seem to sail right through the fields. Aveiro is a fishing village, but it is also the center of a unique business: the collection of seaweed, rich in iodine and used as fertilizer for the nearby fields. The seaweed is harvested by workers who comb the lagoons with wide wooden rakes that are drawn by oxen.

Buçaco Palace, now a hotel

Buçaco is famous for its national park, established by Carmelite friars in the sixth century and revered by the Portuguese as an enchanted forest. Within the park are more than seven hundred species of flowers, plants, and trees, many brought back from the Far East by early Portuguese navigators. A former palace and royal hunting lodge, completed in 1910, is now a hotel, with elegant chandeliers, an unusual staircase, and walls of blue and white tiles known as *azulejos*.

NORTHERN PORTUGAL

The best-known region of northern Portugal is the Costa Verde ("Green Coast"), which reaches along the Atlantic from the town of Espinho in the south to the Spanish border in the north. It stretches east to Vila Real, a land of vineyards, and encompasses three important rivers: Minho, Lima, and Douro.

It was here that the Portuguese nation really started, when Henry of Burgundy was given the county of Portucale and his son, Afonso Henriques, became Afonso I, king of Portugal.

Oporto, the second largest city in Portugal, has a population of over 330,000. Originally it was the town of Portus, which, with Cale, formed the area known as Portucale that was assigned to Henry of Burgundy. So it is widely recognized as the town that gave Portugal its name. The city is perhaps most famous today as the center that produces Port wine. It is essentially a commercial and industrial city, more so even than Lisbon. The inhabitants, proud of its industrious reputation, have a saying: "Coimbra sings, Braga prays, Lisbon shows off, and Oporto works."

Oporto was the birthplace of Henry the Navigator, and many of Henry's expeditions were planned in Oporto. Hundreds of ships returned from Africa, Brazil, and the Far East to Oporto, as well as to Lisbon, establishing the north as an important center of trade and commerce.

Another important factor in Oporto's growth and progress was a trade agreement made with England in 1703. By agreeing that the wine from the region would find a stable market, the signers of the agreement all but insured that Oporto would prosper. At the time of this trade treaty, many people from England moved to Oporto and established a kind of British colony in the region. Shortly thereafter, the wine trade began to flourish and the city became one of the wealthiest in the kingdom.

Oporto is strategically located as a wine center. Not only is it situated on the Atlantic, where it serves as a major port, but it lies at the mouth of the Douro River. The Douro flows from east to west across northern Portugal, watering the many valleys where the grapes are grown. On the uplands alongside the river, the

Vineyards in Oporto

vineyards form patterns of terraces. From these terraces, the grapes are easily brought down to boats along the riverbank, which in turn carry them to Oporto for processing and shipment to all parts of the world.

Viana do Castelo, on the northernmost part of the Portuguese coast, is an old fortress town noted for its Renaissance and Manueline (from Manuel I) architecture. The town lies in the province of Minho, one of the most picturesque and lovingly cultivated in the country. Viana is at the mouth of the Lima River and at the foot of a peak that can be reached by cable car. In the sixteenth century, the town's harbor bustled with ships. Today Viana is known for its pottery, jewelry, embroidery, and other handicrafts. It is particularly noted for its silver filigree, which is very fine and intricately designed. Many of the homes and public buildings are constructed in granite, with iron balconies, decorative windows, and ornate interiors.

Left: Bom Jesus do Monte's Baroque staircase.
Right: A pottery version of Barcelos's legendary rooster

Braga, the fifth largest city in Portugal, is a lovely, ancient town known for its historical and religious significance. Founded by the Romans, it is one of the earliest Christian towns, with the oldest cathedral in Portugal, built during the twelfth century. Outside of town is the Church of Bom Jesus do Monte, which crowns the summit of a densely wooded peak. Beneath the church lie two monumental staircases decorated with statues and fountains.

Barcelos, famous for pottery and handicrafts, is located on the Cávado River about ten miles (sixteen kilometers) inland from the Atlantic. Barcelos has given Portugal its national symbol: the rooster. Legend has it that a pilgrim passing through Barcelos was falsely accused of theft and sentenced to hang. The pilgrim appealed to Saint James. Then he told the judge, who was dining on roast rooster at the time, that the rooster, as proof of the pilgrim's innocence, would stand up and crow. It did, and the pilgrim went free.

Setúbal's harbor, viewed from St. Philip's Castle

BEYOND THE TAGUS

The phrase "beyond the Tagus" commonly refers to the lands that lie to the east of Lisbon, across the broad Tagus River. Since the Tagus flows across Portugal in a southwesterly direction to its mouth at Lisbon, this is a natural dividing line. The towns east of the Tagus are generally spread farther apart than those along the coast. More importantly, they are away from the sea, surrounded by pasturelands and farms, rather than by mountains and forests.

Setúbal, which lies southeast of Lisbon, is the fourth largest city in the country. This is the principal fishing center of the nation, with large processing and canning plants. It also produces oranges and muscatel wine and has a large shipping industry. At the nearby Roman town of Cetóbriga, destroyed by the sea during the fifth century, archaeologists have unearthed many valuable Roman artifacts.

*Évora's landmarks from Roman and Christian times:
the Temple of Diana and the Convent of Loios*

Santarém, to the northeast of Lisbon, is the capital of the
Ribatejo region, a rich, fertile area. The city is built on a hill over
the Tagus River and looks out over a broad plain. From a wide
esplanade known as the *Portas do Sol* (Gate of the Sun), one has a
splendid view of the surrounding country. Santarém is the
agricultural center of the province and is also known for its
campinos, or cowboys. They are very colorful and dashing, dressed
in bright red jackets and wearing green stocking caps with red
tassels.

Évora, not quite 100 miles (161 kilometers) east of Lisbon, is the
most important town in the Alentejo region. The homes in this
community — unique combinations of whitewashed plaster, brick,
and decorative tiles — look like something out of a picture book.
The city is both historically and architecturally rich, containing
the remains of the Roman Temple of Diana, built in the second

Marble quarry in Estremoz

century; the former Convent of Loios, dating from the fifteenth century; and numerous Moorish-style buildings with archways and wrought-iron balconies.

Estremoz, to the northeast of Évora, is a walled city surrounded by seventeenth-century fortifications. Estremoz is noted today for its pottery jars and figurines and for its marble, which has been quarried since Roman times.

Vila Viçosa, whose main street is lined with orange trees and whitewashed houses, is dominated by the enormous palace of the Duke of Bragança. This sixteenth-century edifice makes ample use of the famous Estremoz marble. The palace is said to be haunted by the ghosts of kings, queens, and members of the ancient nobility, and is the setting for many legends about unhappy lovers. King Carlos I spent his last night here before riding to Lisbon the next day, where he was assassinated.

Cape Carvoeiro on Portugal's west coast

Portalegre, near the Spanish border in Upper Alentejo, is noted for its fine tapestries, which are recognized worldwide for their artistry and quality. The tapestry makers of Portalegre use some five thousand different shades of wool. Just to the northeast of Portalegre lies Marvão, with fortified walls jutting high above a giant outcropping of rock. This is the gateway between central Portugal and Spain.

THE ALGARVE

Many people believe that Portugal, like Spain and France, has a southern coast on the Mediterranean. But, as a map clearly shows, Portugal touches no other sea but the Atlantic. Famous for its beaches and summer resorts, the region stretches for some 100 miles (161 kilometers) along Portugal's southern coast. Algarve means "the West" in Arabic, as it lies to the west of most Arabic countries. It is closest of all to Morocco, which is only about 300 miles (483 kilometers) to the south.

Albufeira, one of the Algarve's many resort spots

The Algarve is popular—like southern Spain and France—as a vacation region during the warmer months of the year. It enjoys a balmy climate year-round, though the ocean water is not as warm as that of the Mediterranean. Vacationers from Portugal, other parts of Europe, and North America make the Algarve busy and active from April through September. Many foreigners, too, have settled in the region permanently.

For some five hundred years, the Algarve was dominated by the Moors. They left behind many influences that can be seen today in the Moorish architecture and art of the region.

Faro, the capital of the province, is the southernmost city in Portugal. Its regular population of 28,000 swells considerably during the vacation season. Though Faro is a very old town, few of its structures date back earlier than 1755, when an earthquake destroyed most of the buildings. For centuries, the mountains to the north and the Moorish influence from the south secluded this area from the rest of Portugal. The people developed a distinctive character, partly European and partly Arabic.

A fishing fleet in the harbor of Portimão

Portimão, about forty miles (sixty-four kilometers) west of Faro, is one of the Algarve's major ports. Its harbor is constantly filled with fishing trawlers, small freighters, and yachts. One of the oddities of the town is the creativity of its bakers. For generations they have been baking bread and rolls in the shapes of people, animals, boats, and various symbols.

Lagos, once the capital of the Algarve, lies on the edge of a magnificent bay west of Portimão. The bay is so large that more than four hundred warships were said to have maneuvered there in ancient times. During Portugal's "Golden Age," Lagos was the port where Henry the Navigator's caravels were built.

Steep cliffs and strange rock formations rim the Algarve coast. Many have long tunnels; some have been molded into arches or gateways; and others have been transformed into strange figures, resembling witches and goblins and animals.

Cape St. Vincent, once thought to be the end of the world

Sagres, at the end of a long, rockbound promontory, is known for being the westernmost tip of Europe. Henry the Navigator lived in Sagres for a time and, until recently, it was believed that he built his maritime center there. In ancient times, nearby Cape St. Vincent was considered by mariners to be the end of the world, beyond which there was no other land. The only vessels that even ventured around the cape were those of the Phoenicians and Greeks, and later the Romans, who carefully hugged the coast and did not venture far out to sea. The village is still very small and remote, as it was in Henry's time, surrounded by rugged masses of rock, a few sheltered beaches, and beyond them the seemingly endless stretch of the Atlantic. It is easy, in a place like this, to imagine what Portugal must have been like half a millenium ago, when those first tiny caravels ventured forth on their dangerous voyages, headed for the New World and everlasting glory.

The Douro waters that once saw the launch of great merchant fleets now
power hydroelectric plants (below). The geothermal station in the Azores
(above) is another energy source.

Chapter 5

FERTILE LANDS
AND FAR SEAS

"To the north of the Tagus," wrote Strabo, a Greek geographer and historian who lived during the first century B.C., "stretches Lusitania, inhabited by the most powerful of the Iberian peoples, who repulsed the armies of the Romans for long periods of time and would not give in."

Strabo was not the only writer of that era to comment on the spirit and determination of those early Lusitanians. These same personal characteristics and strengths made it possible for the country's navigators and seamen to undertake voyages that other nations considered foolhardy, if not insane. They also molded the character of the village fishermen who continually braved the sea, from dawn to dusk, without yielding to the weather or flinching in the face of great storms.

By the time ships like the caravel were being designed—ships capable of roving out of sight of land and being navigated scientifically—the Portuguese spirit was equal to the challenge. The early mariners and navigators had the right blend of courage and knowledge and skill to set out on voyages that, indeed, would have been foolhardy for anyone less well-endowed.

These capabilities that were to establish Portugal as the greatest maritime trader of the Middle Ages did not evolve overnight. Before the year 1100, Portuguese *concelhos* were active in several of the small ports along the Atlantic coast. These were trade councils that studied domestic and foreign markets and then encouraged local individuals and groups to develop their skills in handicrafts and agriculture.

The resulting products—from linens, foodstuffs, and raw materials to wines, dried fish, hides, cork, figs, and raisins—were then exported. Products that went to other countries in Europe were largely transported by small sailing vessels, since land transportation was extremely slow and subject to the attacks of robbers and nomadic tribes.

Along with these commercial ventures, the Portuguese slowly and steadily established a navy capable of protecting the country's shipping lanes. As a result, many coastal cities grew not only as commercial ports but as shipbuilding centers.

By the beginning of the fourteenth century, Portugal was widely recognized throughout Europe as a new power—if still a relatively minor one—in the North Atlantic. By the time Portugal's great navigators had discovered Brazil and a new route to India, the country's foreign trade was impressive. Portuguese ships helped to develop new trade routes and bring great wealth to the country through imports of spices and jewels and precious metals.

Much of Portugal's terrain has traditionally been too rocky and hilly for farming.

A DIFFICULT LAND

Portugal of the Middle Ages and later was not nearly as commercially successful on land as it was on the sea. Barely one-third of the country's terrain was suitable for agriculture. The soil was dry, rocky, and hilly. As a result, most farms were small, barely able to sustain individual families. To make matters worse, much of the land was infertile, badly overused by the Romans, Visigoths, Moors, or other early invaders. In a country where many regions were parched and where the rainfall was unreliable, some of the problems could have been solved by irrigation. But the only evidences of irrigation in most cases were the ruins of a few Roman viaducts and water cisterns.

Cattle in the Upper Alentejo plains

Agricultural lands, too, were increasingly used for raising cattle and other livestock, particularly in the central plains. The reason for this was obvious: cattle could be raised at lower cost, with less labor, and could bring higher income than was possible when planting the same acreage in grains or other produce. It seems astonishing that, by the fourteenth century, many of the coastal towns—with small populations and thousands of acres of nearby lands—should have had to *import* grain.

Although Portugal eventually became well known for its wines, such as Port and Madeira and muscatel, the development of the vineyards was slow. Progress was made during the sixteenth century when it became generally recognized that grapes and olives were more profitable than other crops. This discovery further diminished plantings of corn, wheat, and other grains. It came at a time when Lisbon and several other cities and towns were experiencing large population increases. The results were undernourishment and, in several instances, serious famines.

*For centuries Portugal has exported salt and olive oil: mounds of
salt from the Aveiro salt flats (left); olive trees (right).*

FOREIGN TRADE

From about the thirteenth century on, Portugal enjoyed good
trade relationships with western Europe, supplying such goods as
salt, wine, olive oil, wax, honey, leather, and cork. In return,
Portugal received shipments of textiles, dyes, wood, and horses.

Brazil and the African colonies were a source of much wealth,
including cotton, tobacco, dye-wood, ivory, and other highly
profitable exports. The independence of Brazil, however, and the
later decline of colonization seriously affected Portugal's
international trade and economy. As other European nations
developed their own fleets and began ranging the world, Portugal
gradually lost its initial advantage. Today the country continues to
produce and market many excellent—even unique—products. But
its best "resource" is its people, whose affable nature and
considerate ways do much to enhance one of the country's most
rewarding industries: tourism.

AGRICULTURE AND WINES

About one-third of Portugal's total mainland area is devoted to agriculture, which occupies less than 28 percent of the labor force. Grains such as wheat, corn, barley, and rye are among the principal crops for domestic use. These are grown largely in the interior and coastal plains, and to some extent in the upland plateaus. Olive oil is a valuable export, and Portugal is now its fourth largest producer worldwide. Olive trees thrive on the lower slopes of the hills, especially along the northeastern reaches of the Tagus River and in the rolling sections of the Algarve. Along the southern coast are numerous groves of oranges and some other citrus fruits, though few of these are exported.

Nevertheless, Portugal's agriculture is in serious decline today, as more and more workers seek government jobs in the cities. More than half of Portugal's food must be imported today.

Almost 10 percent of the arable land in Portugal is devoted to vineyards. The climate is never too cold and grapes thrive just about anywhere except in the central plains of Alentejo and part of the Algarve where the weather is too warm and dry. There are five major wine regions: the north, along the Douro Valley, where there is more rain and mist than elsewhere; the region around Lisbon; the south, in parts of the Algarve and the Alentejo; the Minho region in the north; and along the Dao River in the northern central section of the country.

The soil in the best producing areas is generally light and sandy, sometimes even gravelly. This makes it easy for the roots of the vines to penetrate, spread, and receive moisture and nutrients. This kind of soil also absorbs and holds warmth from the sun longer than do other types.

Harvesting grapes (left). Quality-testing Port wine (right)

Historically, some Portuguese wines go back to Roman times. The great Roman orator Cicero mentioned the vineyards of Lusitania in the first century B.C. Some three hundred years later, it was recorded that these same types of wines were being shipped to Rome. By the thirteenth century, the vineyards had become so important to the country that they were placed under the king's protection and regulation. It was also decreed then that vineyards be planted on all arable land not suitable for growing grain.

In the middle of the seventeenth century a British syndicate founded a winery in Oporto. This marked the beginning of Port wine, most of which was originally sent to England. The major Portuguese export wines today are Port, Madeira (from the island of Madeira), and muscatel. Very few wines were shipped to the United States until about the 1940s. After that, rosé wines became popular, and have been marketed widely.

Cork trees near Elvas

FOREST PRODUCTS

Although few people think of cork as a forest product, it is exactly that. It is the outer bark of an evergreen species of oak tree that is grown in very few regions outside of Portugal and the northern Mediterranean countries. Portugal supplies about half of all the cork in the world. Cork has been used as an insulating material for spacecraft traveling to the moon and on the first space shuttle. It is also used in nuclear submarines, on jet planes, on the walls and floors of homes, inside the engines of automobiles and trucks, and in home appliances and electronic gear. Despite widespread research, nothing has yet been devised that will replace natural cork and its amazing properties.

Other regularly exported forest products are rosin and turpentine, which are distilled from the sap of evergreens, and pulp for making paper.

Portuguese fishermen laboring at the oars

FISHING

It seems hardly necessary to associate Portugal with fishing, since it is probably the oldest industry in the country, going far back before any recorded history. Since about half of all the cities and towns in Portugal lie close to the sea, their inhabitants have been engaged in fishing for hundreds of years.

Fishing in Portugal is largely a family industry, or, at best, one that involves only closely knit groups. There are few large commercial fishing fleets like those of the Japanese, the Russians, or the Americans. The vessels are still much like the ones used generations ago. Small boats rowed with primitive oars and oarlocks are commonplace. Very few have engines or even outboards. The fishermen, dependent upon each other for their livelihood and often their lives, set out regularly no matter what the weather.

Bringing in the day's catch

At the end of the day, when the boats are brought in, each crew delivers its catch to a central market where the fish are sold at auction. The catch of the day may include a wide variety of fish, from tiny crayfish and shrimp to lobsters, crabs, eels, octopus, squid, sardines, tuna, cod, and whiting. In recent years, shellfish have been in short supply, commanding fat prices. But most of the fish are very reasonably priced, whether destined for local or foreign markets. Portugal has established numerous facilities for processing, canning, and freezing fish for worldwide export.

HANDICRAFTS

Portugal is famous for its glazed tiles, which are brilliantly colored and patterned. They are used widely in exterior

A pottery maker (left). A Caldas da Rainha pottery stall (right)

architecture, as well as for interiors. Pottery making is also one of the country's finest arts. Glazed earthenware from Coimbra was being produced in the thirteenth century by a method handed down through generations. Each region has its own colors and designs for pottery, tiles, and related products. Alcobaça pottery, for example, has a typical dark blue color, while that from Caldas da Rainha is distinguished by its vivid grass green.

The most widely recognized porcelain is that produced by the Vista Alegre factory near Aveiro, which was founded more than 150 years ago. Some is highly decorated. Among the most sought-after examples are very delicate reproductions of flowers, all in their natural sizes and colors.

Fine stoneware, glass, and crystal are produced in certain sections of the country, both for domestic use and for export. The

A Lisbon street vendor selling embroidered tablecloths (left)
The bobbin lace school in Vila do Conde (right)

making of fine crystal has been an art in Portugal since the eighteenth century. One of the earliest furnaces was located at Marinha Grande in 1748 and is still in operation today, as one of the leading glass and crystal producers in Europe.

Portugal has long been famous for its fine linens, tapestries, embroidery work, and carpets. These have been produced down through generations by individuals and families, and only recently by more commercial establishments. Many of these products are regional in origin. Madeira, for example, is noted for its delicate linens and exquisite embroidery. Arraiolos rugs get their name from the town of Arraiolos, where they were first made in the sixteenth century. Today the four rug-making factories in the town use the same materials and methods developed four centuries ago.

The Romans and earlier inhabitants tapped Portugal's mines and quarries.

MINING

Portugal's mining industry is not large, but has been important to the country since its earliest origins. There is evidence, for example, that early tribes in the Alentejo region settled there because it was a source of copper. Copper mining is active there today. Silver was also found in the Alentejo, and tin to the south in the Algarve. Iron, in demand from earliest times and later in the Middle Ages when it was heavily used in architecture, is mined today in northeastern Portugal, near the Spanish border. Tungsten also is mined in north and central Portugal.

Although Portugal has significant mineral wealth for future development, many of the deposits are small or scattered and, except for iron ore, difficult to develop on a large scale.

Building wooden boats in Póvoa de Varzim

SHIPBUILDING

Shipbuilding in Portugal developed into a real art in the fourteenth and fifteenth centuries when the country's sea captains began undertaking long voyages of discovery. The creation of the caravel was one such example. With a wide hull that displaced very little water, and with three main triangular sails hung from long spars, the caravel could be maneuvered easily, despite the direction and force of the wind.

Since the end of World War II, Portuguese shipbuilding has been slowly expanding, along with iron and steel mills. The principal shipbuilding ports are Lisbon and Oporto.

TRANSPORTATION AND COMMUNICATION

During the last few years, Portugal has been improving its major highways. These run mainly from north to south, connecting Oporto, Lisbon, and the Algarve, for example; or from west to east, connecting the major coastal cities with the interior and the main highways into Spain.

Public transportation varies considerably, depending upon the region and the community. Bus transportation is commonplace for commuting from home to work. The railroad system is nationalized and somewhat limited. Modernization and expansion have been planned, but will probably not be in effect for some years.

The national airline, TAP (Air Portugal), and foreign airlines maintain excellent services to most parts of the world from the airport in Lisbon. Other major airports are located at Oporto, Faro, Madeira, and the Azores for both domestic and international flights.

Portugal has developed a reasonably extensive communications system, most of which is under government control. A telephone system with automatic dialing serves most of the country, with connections to other parts of Europe.

Portugal still has far to go in stabilizing and expanding its economy. The government is encouraging any industry that will either increase its exports or reduce its imports. There is excellent potential in tourism, which is being expanded, in the development of food and timber products, and in manufacturing. Portugal is a nation of hard workers, who are used to long hours and relatively modest pay, and who would like to improve their standards of living.

The art of azulejos, as shown in one of the magnificent tile scenes on the walls of Buçaco Palace

Chapter 6

CULTURAL ROOTS
AND ANTIQUITY

It is significant that Portuguese culture started with *love.* Until the thirteenth century, there were no songs, no literature, no art that could be called Portuguese. The cultural elements before that time were imported by the Celts, the Visigoths, the Romans, and the Moors as they invaded the land and established their own ways of life.

Portuguese literature first emerged, in the thirteenth century, in the form of three *cancioneiros*, or songbooks. These were simply romantic laments expressed by maidens longing for their absent lovers. Although these early poems were genuinely Portuguese in their language and expression, they were greatly influenced by the Provençal literature of France. This was quite natural, since Henry of Burgundy, father of Afonso I, the first ruler of Portugal, had come from France with a retinue of French noblemen and intellectuals.

Several of the early Portuguese kings were themselves poets of considerable merit, notably Sancho I, son of Afonso I, and Dinis. Both had been greatly influenced by French troubadors and encouraged the creation of songs and poems in their courts. The mood of these tended to be plaintive, though the structure was quite formal and restrained. The *cantigas*, or songs, were so appealing, however, that for many generations Portuguese was considered "the language of poetry." Even in nearby Spain, poets chose Portuguese instead of Spanish when composing love songs. Alfonso the Wise of Spain, who reigned from 1252 until 1284 and was another royal poet, preferred the Portuguese language to his own when composing verses.

For a time, poetry gave way to chronicles of heroes and great deeds. One of the most popular writers in this new genre was Fernão Mendes Pinto, who wrote about remote and exotic lands and the deeds of Portugal's explorers. He was followed by Gil Vicente, who wrote more than forty plays and is considered the father of Portuguese drama. These writers set the stage for the works of Luís de Camões, who is universally recognized as the greatest figure in Portuguese literature. He has been compared favorably with Miguel de Cervantes and William Shakespeare.

Camões, who lived from 1524 to 1580, wrote an epic poem, *The Lusiads*, telling the story of Vasco da Gama and his daring voyage from Lisbon to India. But this work went far beyond telling a story. Considered the greatest single poem in Portuguese literature, it gave deep insights into the Portuguese character and outlook and foretold the destiny of the nation.

Camões brought a new vitality to lyric poetry and songs, partly because of his own romantic experiences and desires. He was born of a poor family, yet managed to study at the University of

*Luís de Camões,
author of* The Lusiads

Coimbra, where he became familiar with classic literature. He
then fell in love with a lady of the Lisbon court, Dona Caterina,
who became the inspiration for a series of fiery love poems. But,
because he was of humble birth, he was banished from the court
for daring to express love for a lady of the nobility. He served as a
soldier in one of the campaigns against the Moors in North Africa,
where he lost an eye. Upon returning to Lisbon, he was
imprisoned for injuring an official in a street fight.

After his release, Camões consented to serve in India, where he
found great inspiration for *The Lusiads*, which he had already
started to compose. After its publication, he received a meager
pension for his work, but eventually died in poverty and
obscurity—just as his poetry was beginning to receive wide
recognition throughout Europe. The fame of Camões rests on
many other works besides this epic, however. He is widely
admired, too, for lyrics and sonnets that have been called
"flawlessly crafted" and the inspiration of genius.

INSPIRATIONS OF THE SEVENTEENTH CENTURY

One of the most unusual, even mysterious, works of the seventeenth century was *Letters of a Portuguese Nun,* by Mariana Alcoforado. The author was reputed to be a nun at a convent in Beja, although experts now dispute this. The *Letters,* banned by the Church, were written in the form of love letters to a dashing French officer who had deserted his lover. They reveal the passionate desires and frustrations of a brilliant woman in love, but aware of the strict limitations of her calling. Little is known of either the actual author or the beloved officer.

The use of "letters" as a medium became very popular during this literary period. Francisco Manuel de Melo's major work, *Cartas Familiares (Family Letters),* contains five hundred letters that discuss numerous subjects of common concern.

ROMANTICISM

Although Portuguese literature, music, and art did achieve a new kind of independence, they also succumbed to the spirit of romanticism that dominated all of Europe in the nineteenth century. One of the leaders was João Batista de Almeida Garrett, a prolific dramatist, poet, journalist, and orator. He became the recognized leader of the romantic movement in Portugal, although twice forced into exile for his political liberalism. He is still considered one of the greatest of his country's dramatists.

The nineteenth century was rich in writers, though not all of them were romantics. One group of poets—including Antero de Quental and Manuel Junqueiro—rejected romanticism and focused on sociological and philosophical themes.

Another author of significance was Alexandre Herculano, who became Portugal's first romantic novelist. Although he was basically a historian, he also wrote historical novels in the manner of Sir Walter Scott. Three other novelists of note were Júlio Dinis, who created the naturalist novel; Camilo Castelo Branco, who used various themes and approaches; and Eça de Queiros, a powerful realist whose book *The Sin of Father Amaro* has been widely published in English and other languages, as well as in Portuguese. With four other writers, Queiros formed a group known as "The Five," which presided over the literary scene.

The current era in Portuguese letters really dates from the founding of the Republic in 1910. During the twentieth century, much of the important writing has been in literary journals.

THE EMERGENCE AND DEVELOPMENT OF ART

Portuguese art had its origins largely in the architecture left behind by various invaders. Byzantine art flourished prior to the Middle Ages, as did Moorish designs and symbols. The ancient Greek cross, for instance, was a dominant feature, both in design and in floor plans of buildings. Islamic designs dominated some regions until well into the sixteenth century.

The purest form of Portuguese art and design owes much of its beginnings to the sea. During the reigns of Manuel I (1495-1521) and his successor, João III (1521-1557), art and architecture flourished. Much of it was influenced by the Orient and other far places visited by Portuguese ships on voyages of discovery. But gradually many new designs, notably in architecture, began to incorporate such maritime symbols as ropes, coral, dripping seaweed, sailors' buckles, and sails.

*The Manueline style: Lisbon's Hieronymite Monastery (left)
and a detail of Sintra's Pena Palace (right)*

As in most European countries, the first substantial patron of
the arts was the Roman Catholic church, which had become the
official church of Portugal. So influential was Manuel I in
allocating funds and encouraging artistic expression that his name
became synonymous with art. The Manueline style was popular.
Although it was basically a flamboyant Gothic, showing Spanish
and Moorish influence, it acquired certain native characteristics
that set it apart, such as the use of maritime designs and symbols.
One noted artist of this era was Diogo de Arruda.

The Manueline style did not long outlive the king who created
it. It was too magnificent and expensive to survive, and the rulers
who followed Manuel I encouraged simpler forms. Influences
from other countries continued to shape the development of art
and architecture in Portugal, notably from Spain, France, Italy,
and Germany. In the early eighteenth century, for example, a
German architect, Friederich Ludwig, was hired by King João V to

Mafra Monastery (left). Machado de Castro's statue of José I in Lisbon's Black Horse Square, where Carlos I and his heir were assassinated

design a huge monastery and palace in the village of Mafra, northwest of Lisbon. His baroque masterpiece had a considerable influence on contemporary design.

PAINTING AND SCULPTURE

During the Middle Ages, and even later, there were very few paintings or sculptures that were not associated with architecture, religion, or both. The exceptions were portraits or statues of national heroes and members of the royal family that were commissioned by the king or his representatives. A fine example is the great statue of King José I astride his horse that was designed for a public square in Lisbon by the Portuguese sculptor Machado de Castro. He is also noted for sculpture of a completely different dimension: miniatures. He designed some of the country's most valuable nativity figures, all in intricate detail.

Barcelos pottery

Much of the later art originated in small wood carvings or the decoration of tiles, pottery, and porcelains. Most of this artistry was associated more with handicrafts than with fine art. Yet it served to establish patterns of creative development that would evolve in greater works later. Modern Portuguese sculpture tends to be formal and restrained, still evidencing the influence of the days when work was commissioned by the government or king.

In Portuguese painting the emphasis was usually on portraiture or on vast historic scenes commissioned for public buildings, palaces, churches, and monasteries. Many artists showed great talent within the restrictions of their commissions. One of the earliest and greatest was Nuno Goncalves, who painted during the fifteenth century. He was recognized not only for the accuracy of his portraiture of the great personalities of his day but also for his renditions of monks, fishermen, soldiers, and others.

Handcrafted model fishing boats in Nazaré

Other noted painters during the Golden Age were Vasco Fernandes, referred to as the "Great Vasco"; Jorge Afonso, of Lisbon, royal painter to the king; and Frei Carlos, a monk at the monastery of Espinheiro in Évora. After their time, Portuguese art went into a steady decline, its unique style dominated by Italian and other outside influences.

The eighteenth century marked an era of cultural richness, when Lisbon was a center of art, music, and literature. Artists from all over Europe were attracted to the capital during the reign of João V. Portuguese baroque was the popular style, but it was a blend of many styles from other parts of Europe. The major works in architecture, painting, and sculpture were for the most part executed by foreigners. Native artists confined their talents to wood carving, ceramic tiles, and the decorative arts. Some of the most creative achievements were in the designs for tiles.

The nineteenth century produced art that was in keeping with the romantic movement in literature. This was a time, too, when paintings and sculptures from Brazil and other Portuguese colonies were popular. After the turn of the century, however, the constant political turmoil adversely affected artistic creativity. Another restricting factor, especially following the downfall of the royal family, was the lack of funds for commissioning public works of art.

The modern period of art is best represented in the new Center of Modern Art in Lisbon, which has representative showings of the principal contemporary artists. The father of the modern school is recognized as Almada Negreiros, who created, among other works, thirty-foot (nine-meter) tapestries. Other artists of importance are Amadeo de Souza Cardoso, Armando Basta, Carlos Botelho, Noronha da Costa, and Martha Telles.

EDUCATION

Portugal has a universal system of free education, from primary school to the university level. It has been restricted, however, by the shortage of facilities in many localities and the lack of financial assistance in helping to defray living expenses. Children are required to attend school from age six through fourteen.

Historically, few members of the royal family or nobility paid much attention to the education of the people. One exception was the Marquis of Pombal. When he served as prime minister in the eighteenth century, he lent great effort to the cause of educational reform. He became involved, as might be expected, in bitter controversy when he attributed many of Portugal's intellectual deficiencies to the restrictiveness of Jesuit educational programs.

University of Coimbra

As an antidote, he proposed that education be under the control of the government, not the church. He withdrew teaching privileges from the clergy and transferred them to lay professors who were paid by the state. He also founded a School of Commerce and a Royal College of Nobles. One of his greatest achievements was the reform of the University of Coimbra, which modernized the teaching of law and science and helped to make this institution one of the finest in Europe.

It was not until the 1920s that educational reforms were of much benefit to female students in a society that had long been male oriented. But gradually the education of women has led to their successful entry into law, medicine, science, politics, and the arts—as well as higher education itself. This has proved to be a major step forward in the educational system. And it has also characterized a changing outlook for the future in every facet of Portuguese life and thought.

The face of Portugal has seen the ravages of time and the promises of the future.

Chapter 7

THE QUIET FACES OF

PORTUGAL

How can you tell if a person is Portuguese? What is it about the Portuguese that distinguishes them from other nationalities? The truth is that you could meet one, two, or a dozen Portuguese and have no clear idea of their nationality. They are Iberian, being from the Iberian Peninsula. They are Latin, in that the country has roots in Rome. They also have traces of Greek, French, English, German, and North African.

The Portuguese, like the Spanish, have the heritage of many peoples. The population today is described as homogeneous. That is, it is well blended and quite uniform. Nevertheless, there are many physical types among the native citizens of the country. Some, like the inhabitants of rural areas in the north, may have blond hair and blue eyes, their heritage from the Germanic Visigoths. Others, particularly from the Algarve, may have the dark look of the Moors. Many may display characteristics of the Romans, the Greeks, or Brazilians who migrated to Portugal.

The Portuguese have yet another dimension that is both fascinating and mysterious. Some have the blood of kings and queens in their veins. Others come from long lines of peasants or fishermen. Which are which? Physically, it is impossible to tell. And from the standpoint of current occupation, economic position, or social stature, it would be just as difficult to analyze. For the most successful citizens of Portugal are often the ones who have lifted themselves by their own bootstraps, as the saying goes. They have lived with poverty, worked hard to emerge from it, and accomplished objectives that have changed their lives.

Others, of course, have sought no change and have been satisfied to pursue the same fields of endeavor that were their endowments at birth. This is often true in the case of fishermen who have lived all their lives in the same villages where their forebears were fishermen before them.

Portugal has absorbed a broad mixture of peoples into its society, including a large number of Africans and Asians after the 1974 revolution. Although more than 95 percent of the people adhere to Roman Catholicism, the official religion, there is complete freedom of worship. Catholics, Protestants, Jews, Muslims, and others worship as they please, with no interference or pressure.

FAMILY RELATIONSHIPS

The family has always been the nucleus of Portuguese life. To some extent, this family bond was formed and strengthened in ancient times when people banded together to resist invaders.

The family is still vital in most communities in Portugal, even in the cities and larger towns. Family members are very close—

Left: A father and his children in Mafra. Right: A fisherman's family in Oporto

not just immediate relatives, but uncles, aunts, in-laws, and distant cousins. On a Sunday or holiday, family groups can be seen enjoying themselves at the beach, in picnic grounds, driving along the highways, or browsing through the little stalls at a roadside shopping fair.

When a man and woman are wed, they automatically "adopt" their in-laws as part of their new family. Thus, over a period of years, a family group can become quite large and yet be strongly knit. When a foreign journalist criticized the Portuguese for not having more "public spirit" and performing more voluntary services in the community, he was admonished for having such an idea. The Portuguese, he was told, simply do not have room for public services of this kind—not after they have contributed all of their time and effort to family members who may have problems and needs that require sympathetic attention.

A girl in Oporto dressed for the São Pedro festival (left). In Tomar's Tabuleiros Festival, young girls parade through the streets bearing platters piled high with bread loaves (right).

FAIRS AND FESTIVALS

Travelers from abroad who visit Portugal are likely to encounter numerous street fairs in the towns and country festivals in the more rural areas. Street fairs occur at any time of the week and country festivals only on weekends or holidays. Many of them are sponsored by local churches, while some may be backed by merchants seeking to attract more business.

The more lavish fairs have games, fortune-tellers, a colorful procession, and fireworks. Some festivals are related to religious events, and feature costumed religious dramas. Others may be tied in with historical dates, requiring not only costumes of the period but the preparation of certain appropriate dishes.

What makes these occasions typically Portuguese is that there is very little boisterous activity or rudeness. The Portuguese are a

A friendly fish merchant in Viana do Castelo

quiet people, which well befits the mellow, poetic nature of their language. They laugh and smile often, yet in a most natural way. They are affable with strangers, often offering to share something or lend a helping hand. At the same time, they never push their friendliness. If there is one common opinion that foreign visitors come away with, it is that they always felt comfortable, whether lost in a crowd or rubbing elbows with only a few individuals.

The Portuguese are fond of shaking hands, not only when meeting someone, but on perfectly insignificant occasions. A customer might shake the hand of a store owner after a purchase. A merchant might do the same with the postman who is delivering the mail. It is perfectly proper—and appreciated—to shake the hand of a restaurant manager as you leave, or a bank teller after you have made a deposit, or a friend whom you already have seen several times that same day.

One of Lisbon's many sidewalk cafes

SMALL TALK AND HOT COFFEE

The Portuguese have one common, perpetual hobby: being neighborly. Their cities and towns are crowded, but they live in this close proximity largely by choice. It gives them a better opportunity to be communicative. Walking down the narrow streets of the Alfama, the oldest section of Lisbon, one quickly notices that everyone is talking. People stand in little knots of three or four, peer upward from basement steps they are tidying, gaze down from windows and balconies overhead, and chat.

Along Lisbon's broad Avenida da Liberdade on a sunny day, residents are perched beside minitables on the mosaic sidewalks sipping tiny glasses of black coffee. As they sit outside the small cafes or *pastelarias* (pastry shops), they are in a fine position to greet friends, acquaintances, or relatives who may be walking along, enjoying the sights and sounds of the capital. Everyone is an actor in this passing drama.

Portugal offers a variety of delicious pastries to complement hearty meals.

Inside the restaurants and cafes people gather in much the same way. The Portuguese love to eat, and have many tasty dishes to offer their guests. Yet they seem to go out to dine as much for the conversation and camaraderie as for the food. At noon, the shops and businesses close for two or three hours. In many tropical lands a similar siesta period is used to escape the hottest hours of the day. In Portugal, however, where the climate is comfortable and temperate, the midday break is a social one.

Lunch is usually the main meal of the day. Wine is consumed at both lunch and dinner, but usually in moderate amounts, for most people are conservative drinkers. Vegetables and fish are popular, with less emphasis on meats than in most Western countries. The big moment of any meal is near the end—the pastries, puddings, custards, and other sweets. One of the favorites is a light, fluffy dessert made of egg whites and coated with the yolks blended with sugar. Most people will conclude a repast with a small glass of rich black coffee or with coffee mixed with hot milk.

Fish dinners (left) and caldo verde *(right) are not to be missed.*

Some national and regional specialities that Portuguese people enjoy are quite simple, having originated in small farms or fishing villages, rather than in palaces and manor houses. *Caldeirada* is a good example. It is a fisherman's stew, a delicious blend of fish, vegetables, and herbs. It is somewhat like the *paella* that is so popular in Spain. A counterpart is *cozido à Portuguesa*, a boiled dish of lamb or beef, onions, potatoes, and other vegetables.

If there is a "national dish," it is probably *caldo verde*, a thick hearty soup made with potatoes and cabbage. The secret lies in the way the cook blends the ingredients so that the flavor is subtle. For those who cannot decide whether to have meat or fish, the local chefs have numerous offerings. One is *porco à Alentejana*, a recipe that combines pork and clams in an appetizing sauce.

Whether at mealtime or at work, at home or in public, people of all ages tend to be somewhat formal in dress. This habit has

Festival dress (left) is stunning, but rural women's everyday wear (right) is a sight to behold as well.

changed considerably with the younger generation and in the more cosmopolitan sections of the cities. However, it is still quite commonplace to see well-groomed businessmen in dark suits, with shoes polished to a mirrorlike finish. In the rural areas, it is not uncommon to see farm women in dresses that seem to be designed for going to church rather than to work. They may be wearing bright blue blouses and white aprons over dark skirts. Some wear scarves or flaunt little black felt hats that are round and flat, called "porkpies."

One reason for the fanciful dress is that the people of the outlying regions typically like to add a note of fun to their work. During harvesting seasons they dress up, make a social event out of the gathering of crops, and often hold simple contests. These might be to see who can shuck the most corn, card the most flax, or pick the most beans in a given period of time.

The season of the grape harvest is also an occasion for celebration.

PEOPLE AND MUSIC

Certain kinds of harvests are occasions for entire villages to work hard but also to engage in communal fun. One such event is the gathering of olives, which involves beating the trees so the fruit falls into gathering cloths and baskets. Another is the cutting of grapes, especially in the rich vineyards along the Douro River. Whole families and groups of villagers march to the scene, often in colorful costumes. An important element is the music—guitars and fiddles, tambourines and reed pipes. Along the way they may be joined by barking dogs, crowing roosters, quacking ducks, and small children beating time with sticks and makeshift drums.

Music in the small towns is likely to consist of folk tunes played by street musicians. It varies from lively tunes to slow, sad ballads. Then there is the unique music of certain tradespeople announcing their wares or services. The knife grinder is typical. A plaintive wailing tune heard in the distance may be one of these

Cavaleiros in Portuguese bullfights dress in ornate, seventeenth-century costumes.

men with a portable grindstone, making his rounds. The instrument he uses, though, is not a flutelike instrument at all, but a kind of primitive mouth organ.

The bullfight is another event that calls for music, notably the *pasodoble.* This is a kind of march that heralds the beginning of the contest and builds up excitement. Kettledrums and trumpets are often an integral part of the proceedings.

A bullfight, Portuguese style, is much different from its Spanish counterpart in that the bulls are never killed. In this respect, it is more like a Western rodeo, featuring dashing *cavaleiros* on horseback. Dressed in colorful seventeenth-century costumes, they ride back and forth in front of the bull. After the *cavaleiros* have performed, all to the sound of trumpets, a team of *forcados* appears from the sidelines, dressed in gaily colored waistcoats and breeches. They attempt to bring the bull to standstill—called "bulldogging," as in the rodeo—by grasping its horns and wrestling it to the ground.

Two musicians rehearse in an Algarve restaurant.

Finally, the matador appears on foot, a classic type of bullfighter with a red, swirling cape. He puts the bull, as well as himself, through a series of graceful, traditional paces. In the end, instead of killing the bull with a sword, he closes in, gives the animal a slap on the head, and is done.

The most unique and characteristic form of music in Portugal is the fado. The fado (which means "fate") is a sad, throaty ballad sung—usually by a woman—to the tune of two guitars. Traditionally, one is a Spanish instrument, the other Portuguese, resembling an enlarged banjo with a very delicate tone.

The best known and most characteristic type of fado is the mournful, almost eerie, lament that is sung late in the evening in the small, older cafes of Lisbon. The ballads speak of lost loves and sorrow and the far away and long ago. They deal with the heartbreak of separated sweethearts or of unrequited love. In this

they have their roots in the ancient love poems that were
Portugal's first literary masterpieces.

No one really knows exactly how the fado came into being.
Some say that these ballads, like the love poems of the Middle
Ages, evolved from the songs of Portuguese seamen who longed
for their families or sweethearts. Others have traced the songs
back to the days of the Moors. And a few believe that the
undulating rhythms of the fado took their form from the simple
songs of Portuguese fishermen as they rode the Atlantic swells in
their sturdy, high prowed boats.

No matter what the origins, the fado is an appropriate symbol
for Portugal itself. It combines so many of the elements that
characterize this small nation: dignity, mystery, charm, antiquity,
and the endless striving for personal understanding and
communication.

MAP KEY

Abrantes	C1	Deserta Grande		Penamacor	B2
Agueda	B1	(island)	h12	Peniche	C1
Albergaria-a-Velha	B1	Douro (Duero) (river)	B1,2	Peso da Régua	B2
Albufeira	D1	Elvas	C2	Pinhal Nova	f10
Alcabideche	f9	Entre Minho e Douro		Pinhel	B2
Alcácer do Sal	C1	(region)	B1	Pombal	C1
Alcochete	f10	Esposende	B1	Ponte de Sor	C1
Alenquer	C1	Estarreja	B1	Portalegre	C2
Alentejo (region)	C,D2	Estremadura (region)	C,D1	Portimão	D1
Algarve (region)	D1,2	Estremoz	C2	Porto (Oporto)	B1
Alhos Vedros	f9	Evora	C2	Pôrto de Mós	C1
Aljezur	D1	Fafe	B1	Porto Santo (island)	g12
Aljustrel	D1	Faro	D2	Póvoa de Varzim	B1
Almada	C1,f9	Ferreira do Alentejo	C1	Proença-a-Nova	C2
Almargem	f9	Ferreira do Zêzere	C1	Redondo	C2
Almeirim	D1	Figueira da Foz	B1	Reguengos Monsaraz	C2
Almodóvar	D1	Funchal	h12	Rio Maior	C1
Alpiarca	C1	Fundão	B2	Sa. da Estrela	
Alter do Chão	C2	Grândola	C1	(mountains)	B1,2
Alverca	f9	Guadiana (river)	C1,D2	Sabor (river)	B2
Ardila (river)	C2	Guarda	B2	Sacavém	f9
Arraiolos	C2	Guimarães	B1	Sacovém	f9
Aveiro	B1	Idanha-a-Nova	C2	Sada (river)	C,D1
Barca de Alva	B2	Ilhavo	B1	Santana	h12
Barcarena	f9	Lagoa	D1	Santarém	C1
Barcelos	B1	Lagos	D1	São João das Lampas	f9
Barreiro	C1,f9	Lamego	B2	São Vicente	h11
Bay of Setúbal	C1	Leiria	C1	Seixal	f9
Beira (region)	B1,2	Lezirias (region)	f10	Serpa	D2
Beja	C2	Lima (river)	B1	Sertã	C1
Belas	f9	Lisbon (Lisboa)	C1,f9	Setúbal	C1
Belém	f9	Loulé	D1	Setúbal Bay	C1
Berlengas Is. (island)	C1	Loures	f9	Sezimbra	C1
Braga	B1	Lousã	B1	Silves	D1
Bragança	B2	Machico	h12	Sines	D1
Caldas da Rainha	C1	Madeira (islands)	g,h11,12	Sintra	f9
Calheta	h11	Mafra	C1	Sôr (river)	C1,2
Caminha	B1	Mangualde	B2	Sorraia (river)	-C1,2
Campo Maior	C2	Marinha Grande	C1	Soure	B1
Cantanhede	B1	Matozinhos	B1	Tamega (river)	B1,2
Caparica	f9	Mertola	D2	Tavira	D2
Cape Mondego	B1	Minho (river)	A,B1	Tagus (Tejo) (river)	C1,2
Cape Roco	f9	Mira (river)	D1	Tomar	C1
Cape St. Vincent	D1	Miranda do Douro	B2	Torres Novas	C1
Carnaxide	f9	Mirandela	B2	Torres Vedras	C1
Cartaxo	C1	Moita	f10	Trancoso	B2
Cascais	C1,f9	Monchique	D1	Trás-os-Montes	B2
Cascais Bay	f9	Monchique (mountains)	D1	Túa (river)	B2
Castanheira de Pêra	B1	Mondego (river)	B1,2	Vagos	B1
Castelo Branco	C2	Montalegre	B2	Valença	A1
Castelo de Vide	C2	Montelavar	f9	Viana do Alentejo	C1
Castro Daire	B2	Montemor-o-Novo	C1	Viana do Castelo	B1
Castro Merim	D2	Montijo	C1,f10	Vila da Feira	B1
Castro Verde	D1	Moura	C2	Vila de Rei	C1
Cavado (river)	B1,2	Nazaré	C1	Vila do Conde	B1
Chanca (river)	D2	Nisa	C2	Vila Franca de Xira	C1
Chaves	B2	Odemira	D1	Vila Nova de Foz Coa	B2
Cheleiros	f9	Odivelas	f9	Vila Nova de Gaia	B1
Coa (river)	B2	Oeiras	f9	Vila Nova de Milfontes	D1
Coimbra	B1	Olhão	D2	Vila Real	B2
Colares	f9	Olivais	f9	Vila Real de Sto. António	D2
Coruche	C1	Oporto (Porto)	B1	Vila Viçosa	C2
Covilhã	B2	Ourique	D1	Vinhais	B2
Cuba	C2	Ovar	B1	Viseu	B2
		Pampilhosa do Botão	B1	Vouga (river)	B1,2
		Penafiel	B1	Zezere (river)	B2

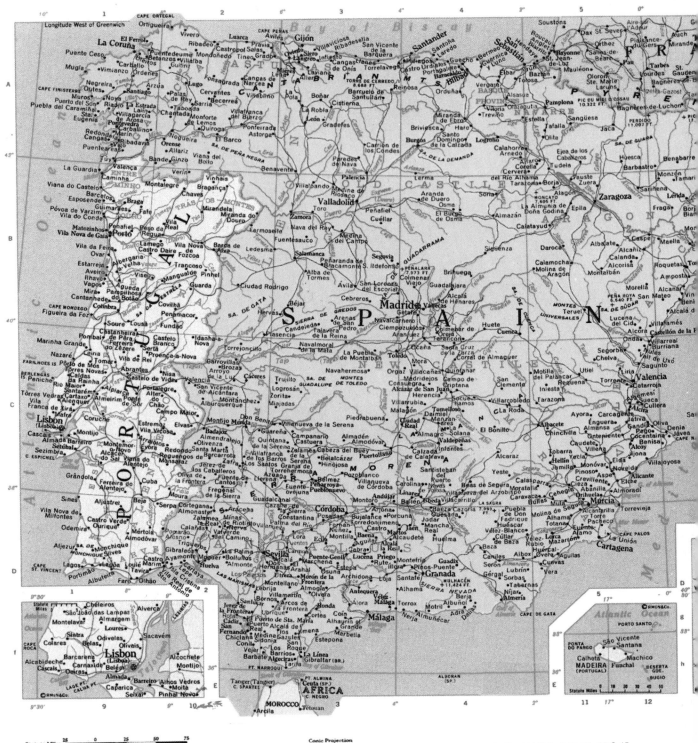

Conic Projection

Statute Miles

Kilometers

MINI-FACTS AT A GLANCE

GENERAL INFORMATION

Official Name: *República Portuguesa* (Portuguese Republic)

Capital: Lisbon

Official Language: Portuguese. Like Spanish, Portuguese is one of the Romance languages that developed from Latin.

Government: Portugal has been a republic since the overthrow of the monarchy in 1910. Its constitution, adopted in 1976, grants freedom of speech, religion, and the press. Citizens eighteen years and older may vote.

Laws are made by a 263-member Parliament elected to four-year terms. The president is elected for a five-year term. The president appoints a prime minister — usually the leader of the party with the most seats in Parliament.

Portugal is divided into twenty-two districts, each run by a governor and a district legislature.

The Supreme Court is the highest court. There are also four lower courts of appeal and a variety of district and lower courts.

In 1975 Portugal held its first free elections in over fifty years. Fourteen political parties participated. The Socialist Party received the highest number of votes. The next three leading parties were the Popular Democratic party, the Social Democratic Center, and the Communist party.

Religion: Most of the Portuguese who practice a religion are Roman Catholics. Followers of other creeds are few; however, there are small groups of Jews, Muslims, and Protestants.

Flag: The flag has a band of green on the left, which stands for hope, and red on the right, which symbolizes the blood of Portugal's heroes. The coat of arms that appears on the flag shows castles, shields, and armillary sphere of medieval and Renaissance times.

National Anthem: *"A Portugesa"* ("The Portuguese") (words by Lopes de Mendonca, 1890; tune by Alfredo Keil)

Money: The unit of currency is the escudo, which is made up of 100 centavos. In September 1985, one United States dollar was worth approximately 168 escudos.

Weights and Measures: The metric system is the legal standard.

Population: 1985 estimate—10,081,000; distribution, 60 percent rural, 40 percent urban; density, 246 persons per sq. mi. (96 per km²)

Major Cities:

Lisbon 817,627
Oporto. 330,199
Setúbal. 76,812
Coimbra 71,782
Braga 65,008
Vila Nova de Gala 60,962
Barreiro. 50,745
Funchal 48,638
Almada 41,468
(Population figures from 1981 census)

GEOGRAPHY

Highest Point: Estrela, in Serra da Estrela, 6,545 ft. (1,993 m)

Lowest Point: Sea level

Mountains: The highest mountains are in the Serra da Estrela range. Peaks there rise more than 6,000 ft. (1,829 m). In the northwest the mountains of Minho Province are surmounted by the Serra do Larouco, 5,003 ft. (1,525 m).

Rivers: The Douro and the Tagus rivers cross Portugal from east to west. The Douro empties into the Atlantic at Oporto. The Tagus flows into the ocean at Lisbon. The Guadiana forms part of Portugal's boundary with Spain in the southeast.

Climate: The climate ranges from cool, damp weather in the north to a drier, Mediterranean-type weather in the south. The central region has the greatest extremes of temperature. July and August are sunny everywhere. Temperatures range from 70° F. in July (21° C) to 50° F. (10° C) in January. Annual precipitation averages 20 to 40 in. (51 to 102 cm).

Greatest Distances: North to south—350 mi. (563 km)
East to west—125 mi. (201 km)

Area: 35,553 sq. mi. (92,082 km²), including the Azores and Madeira island groups. The mainland, excluding the islands—34,340 sq. mi. (88,941 km²)

Trees: One-third of the country is heavily wooded with rich forests of pine, oak, and eucalyptus. Cork trees are also prevalent. Deciduous trees tend to be Atlantic varieties, whereas evergreens for the most part are native to Mediterranean and African countries. Both cultivated and wild olives flourish.

Fish: The sardine industry is of major importance to Portugal's economy. Cod and tuna are also abundant. Shellfish are found on the northern rocky coasts and oyster beds in the Ria de Aveiro and estuaries of the Sado and Tagus rivers.

Animals: Wild goats, wild pigs, and deer are found in the mountains, wolves in the Serra da Estrela, and lynx in the Alentejo. Foxes, rabbits, and Iberian hare are common. Game birds include quail, snipe, woodcock, and red partridge.

EVERYDAY LIFE

Food: Portuguese meals are copious, tasty, and wholesome. *Caldeirada*, or fisherman's stew, is found everywhere; it is a blend of fish, vegetables, and herbs. *Cozido à Portuguesa* is made of lamb or beef, onions, potatoes, and other root vegetables. *Caldo verde* consists of a stock of mashed potatoes to which green Galician cabbage, finely shredded, is added, together with olive oil and slices of black pudding. *Porco à Alentejana* combines pork and clams in an appetizing sauce.

Housing: In general the building of houses in Portugal is financed privately, though low-cost houses for white-collar employees, union members, and civil servants are built with government funds. A special type of low-cost housing is available to fishermen's families.

Holidays:

January 1, New Year's Day
February 11, Carnival Day
April 25, Liberty Day
May 1, Labor Day
June 6, Corpus Christi
June 10, Portugal Day
June 13, Feast of Saint Anthony (Lisbon only)
August 15, Feast of the Assumption
October 5, Proclamation of the Republic
November 1, All Saints' Day
December 1, Restoration of Independence
December 8, Immaculate Conception
December 25, Christmas Day

Culture: Portugal is a country of festivals. On saints' days religious processions are colorful; other celebrations include folk dancing, bullfights, and fireworks.

Folk songs range from lively dance tunes called chulas and viras to sad songs accompanied by guitar called fados.

The Golden Age of Portuguese art began in the fifteenth century, just as Portugal was beginning to emerge as a world power. The art and architecture of the period from the 1400s to the 1600s is called the Manueline style, named for King Manuel I (reigned 1495-1521), who sponsored many artists.

The invaders of Portugal—the Romans, Moors, and Spaniards—have all left their influences on the art and architecture of the country. Another major influence has been the sea, which appears as motifs in painting and folk art as well as in literature.

Sports and Recreation: Folk songs, bullfights, and soccer are the leading recreational activities of Portugal. Unlike bullfights in Spain and Latin America, however, in Portugal the bulls are not killed.

Communication: The government owns and operates the telephone, telegraph, and postal systems. Portuguese often watch TV in public places such as taverns, restaurants, and stores. However, there are more than 1.3 million TV sets in use and over 1.5 million radios. One of the immediate results of the military coup of 1974 was the abolition of press censorship. There are over thirty newspapers in Portugal, of which more than half are published in Lisbon.

Transportation: Portugal has over 18,500 miles (29,773 km) of roads, of which over 60 percent are paved. Automobiles, buses, and streetcars provide much of the transportation in cities, but in rural areas oxcarts, horses, or mules are still used.

The government owns and operates the airlines and railroads. Regular services connect Lisbon with the major cities of the world. The country has an extensive railroad network with about 2,200 mi. (3,540 km) of lines.

Schools: Portugal's educational system is weak compared with that of most western European countries; about a fifth of the people cannot read or write. Although children are required by law to attend school between the ages of six and fourteen, many actually leave before that age. Many sections of the country do not have high schools, and children are needed to work on farms.

There are ten universities, four of which were opened after the 1974 revolution. Lisbon University has more than 18,000 students. Fewer than 2 percent of the people have the benefits of a higher education. Higher education comprises two systems: education in traditional and new universities, and that provided in regional polytechnic institutes offering two- or three-year courses in scientific, technical, and practical training.

Health: Portugal has both public and private hospitals. There are dispensaries and clinics all over the country for the care of new mothers and infants. Special institutes include a school of tropical medicine, a rehabilitation facility for the disabled near Lisbon, a sanatorium in the northern mountains, and a cancer hospital and research unit in Lisbon. Ancient scourges like leprosy have been almost wiped out, but there still is a leper colony.

ECONOMY AND INDUSTRY

Principal Products:
Agriculture: Almonds, corn, figs, grapes, lemons, limes, olives, oranges, rice, wheat

Fishing: Cod, sardines, tuna

Manufacturing: Clothing, cork products, food products, leather goods, linens, metals and machinery, petroleum products, pottery, ships, textiles, wines, copperware, tiles, glassware, jewelry

IMPORTANT DATES

1000s B.C.—Phoenicians establish settlements in what is now Portugal

100s B.C.—Portugal becomes part of the Roman Empire

400s A.D.—Visigoths invade and drive out the Romans

711—Moors invade Iberian peninsula; retain foothold until tenth century

700s to 800s—Pelagus leads the reconquest from Asturias; by the ninth century the region of Portucale, north of the Mondego, has been liberated

1139—Afonso Henriques proclaims himself King Afonso I and defeats Moors

1143—Spain recognizes Portugal's independence

1249—Moors finally driven out from the Algarve

1279-1325—King Dinis I founds the University of Coimbra and establishes Portuguese as the official language

1373—First Treaty of Alliance with England (signed in London)

1385 — Victory over the Castilians at Aljubarrota

1386 — Treaty of Windsor with England

1415 — Beginning of Portuguese expansion

1481-95 — João II is king; Bartolomeu Dias rounds Cape of Good Hope (1488)

1495-1521 — Manuel I on the throne; Vasco da Gama discovers sea route to India (1498); Pedro Álvares Cabral lands in Brazil (1500); Magellan's ship is first to circumnavigate the globe, 1519-22

1578 — King Sebastião killed in Morocco; his death marks the end of Portuguese supremacy

1580 — Philip II of Spain invades Portugal and is proclaimed King Felipe I

1640 — Uprising against Spain; Duke of Braganca becomes João IV

1668 — Spain recognizes Portugal's independence

1703 — Britain and Portugal sign the Methuen Treaty and a trade treaty facilitating shipping of Port wine to England

1755 — Lisbon destroyed by an earthquake

1793 — Portugal joins the first coalition against Revolutionary France

1807 — French invasion under Junot; the royal family goes into exile in Brazil

1808 — Landing of first detachments of British troops, with Wellington in command

1810 — Wellington victorious at Buçaco; last major battle on Portuguese soil in the Peninsular Campaign

1822 — Brazil becomes independent

1834 — Civil war ends in favor of Dom Pedro, with Convention of Evoramonte

1890 — British ultimatum defeats Portugal's plans for colonies in central Africa

1899 — Treaty of Windsor with England

1908—Assassination of King Carlos I and the heir to the throne

1910—Manuel II flees to exile in England; proclamation of First Republic

1910-26—Republic is most unstable political organization in western Europe; Salazar begins rise to power—appointed minister of finance in 1928, prime minister in 1932; he restores economic and political stability but in 1933 promulgates a new constitution.

1926-32—Period of military dictatorship

1968—Salazar suffers a stroke; Marcello Caetano succeeds him

1970—Salazar dies; his successor, Caetano, continues a ruinous, unpopular antiguerrilla war in Africa.

1974—Armed forces movement seizes power

1974-75—Portuguese possessions in Africa attain independence

1975—First free general elections in over fifty years

1976—General Romalho Eanes elected president of the Republic

IMPORTANT PEOPLE

Jorge Afonso, sixteenth-century painter to King Manuel I

Mariana Alcoforado (1640-1723), author of *Letters of a Portuguese Nun*

João Batista de Almeida Garrett (1799-1854), revived art of the drama, chief lyric poet of the early 1800s

Baltasar Álvares (1550-1624), builder of rectangular churches

Pedro Álvares Cabral (1460?-1526?), discovered Brazil in 1500

Diogo de Arruda, the most original Manueline artist; used marine and nautical themes

Francisco de Arrunda, architect of Lisbon's Belem Tower (1516-21); embellished Gothic design with Moorish motifs

Boytac (1490-1520), French architect who designed first Manueline building, the Church of Jesus at Setúbal, and Guarda Cathedral

Teófilo Braga (1843-1924), first president of the Portuguese Republic, 1910

Marcello Caetano (1906-80), prime minister, 1968-74

Luís de Camões (1524-80), greatest Portuguese poet, author of *The Lusiads*, the story of Vasco da Gama

Frei Carlos, sixteenth-century monk and Golden Age painter who worked at the monastery of Espinheiro in Évora

António Óscar de Fragoso Carmona (1869-1951), overthrew government in military coup in 1926; president, 1926-51

Camilo Castelo Branco (1826-90), author of *Fatal Love*

Antonio F. de Castilho (1800-75), poet, author of *Amore Melancholia*

João and Diogo de Castilho, early sixteenth-century architects who worked in Lisbon, Tomar, and Coimbra

Nicolas Chanterene, Renaissance master sculptor of Coimbra school

Christopher Columbus (1451-1506), Genoese navigator married to a Portuguese; discovered the West Indies and Central America

Bartolomeu Dias (1450?-1500), explorer who reached Cape of Good Hope in 1488

Dinis I (1239-1325), king and poet who imposed the Portuguese language as the offical language of the country

Júlio Dinis, nineteenth-century writer of naturalistic novels

Gil Eanes, first explorer to round North Africa's Cape Bojador, the farthest point then known to Europeans, in 1434

José Maria Eça de Queiros (1845-1900), leading realistic novelist of Portugal, author of *The Sin of Father Amaro*

Vasco Fernandes (1480-1543), master painter of the Viseu school

Mateus Fernandes, built unfinished chapel with exuberant decoration near Batalha

Cristóvão de Figueiredo, sixteenth-century Manueline painter who worked in French Impressionist style

João Franco (1855-1929), prime minister 1906-7, a conservative dictator

Vasco da Gama (1469?-1524), navigator, first to sail around Africa to the East

Olivier de Gand, fifteenth-century Flemish architect; sculpted the wood altarpiece at Coimbra cathedral

Nuno Gonçalves, Flemish painter who came to Portugal in late fifteenth century; famous for the St. Vincent polyptych

Henry of Burgundy (1057?-1112), French nobleman who assisted the king of Spain in driving the Moors out of Portugal

Henry the Navigator (died 1460), encouraged ship captains, including Vasco da Gama, to go on voyages of exploration and discovery

Alexandre Herculano (1810-87), romantic novelist; author of four-volume history of Portugal

Houdart, sixteenth-century Renaissance sculptor of realistic statuary; grand master of the Coimbra school

João IV (1605-56), formerly Duke of Bragança, resisted Spanish invasion in 1460

Guerra Junqueiro (1850-1923), satirical poet, author of *Old Age of the Eternal Father*

Gregório Lopes, sixteenth-century painter of life at the Manueline court

Joachim Machado de Castro (1731-1822), sculptor of statue of King José I and of nativity figures

Ferdinand Magellan (1480?-1521), captain of ship that completed first circumnavigation of the globe, 1519-21

Francisco Manuel de Melo (1611-66), author of *Cartas Familiares* ("Family Letters")

Fernão Mendes Pinto (1380-1460), author of *Peregrinations,* relating explorers' exotic adventures

Almada Negreiros, father of the modern school of art; creator of thirty-foot tapestries

Master Pero, fourteenth-century creator of funerary art in Oporto

Fernando Pessoa (1885-1935), poet, author of *Maritime Odes*

Marquis of Pombal (1699-1782), powerful premier, 1750-77; promoted economic development; rebuilt Lisbon after the 1755 earthquake

José Régio, twentieth-century poet, author of *Poems of God and the Devil*

Aquilino Ribeiro, twentieth-century regional author

Jean de Rouen, French Renaissance sculptor who settled in Portugal and excelled in altarpieces and reliefs

António de Oliveira Salazar (1889-1970), prime minister appointed in 1932; responsible for 1933 constitution, but ruled as virtual dictator until 1968

António de Spínola, elected president 1974, granted independence to Guinea-Bissau, Mozambique, Angola, and Cape Verde Islands colonies

Filippo Terzi (1520-97), Italian architect who arrived in Portugal in 1576 and designed in the classical style

Miguel Torga, twentieth-century regional author

Gaspar Vaz (died 1568?), master painter of the Viseu school

Gil Vicente (1470-1536?), first great Portuguese playwright, wrote forty-four plays and religious dramas

António Vieira (1608-1697), Jesuit writer of sermons and letters; missionary in Brazil

Domingos Vieira (1660-78), portrait painter in classical period

Viriatus (died 139 B.C.), popular Lusitanian warrior and chief who resisted Roman invasion in 147 B.C.

Jean d'Ypres, fifteenth-century sculptor who carved wood altarpiece at Coimbra cathedral with Olivier de Gand

INDEX

Page numbers that appear in boldface type indicate illustrations.

About the Authors

Wilbur Cross, a professional writer and editor, is the author of some 25 nonfiction books and several hundred magazine articles. His subjects range widely from travel and foreign culture to history, sociology, medicine, business, adventure, biography, humor, education, and politics. Mr. Cross worked for several years as a copywriter and was an associate editor at *Life* magazine.

Esther Cross has assisted her husband with numerous books and magazine articles. She coauthored with him *A Guide to Unusual Vacations*, covering interesting locations in the United States. Most of her time now is devoted to real estate, being a partner in a Bronxville, New York, firm.

The Crosses have traveled extensively in Latin America and Europe, including Spain and Portugal. The parents of four daughters, they live in Westchester County, New York.

INDEX

Acknowledgments—Excerpt from *The Patton Papers*, edited by Martin Blumenson. Copyright ©1974 by Martin Blumenson. Reprinted by permission of Houghton Mifflin Co. All rights reserved. Our sincere thanks to the Memphis Belle Memorial Association, Inc. in Memphis, Tennessee, for use of their photographs and information.

A 1
B 2
C 3
D 4
E 5
F 6
G 7
H 8
I 9
J 0

CLOCKWISE FROM ABOVE: MANILA, PHILIPPINES—U.S. military cemetery. *Photo George Hall/Woodfin Camp and Associates, Inc.* NORMANDY, FRANCE—U.S. military cemetery overlooking Omaha Beach, the site of the Allied invasion during Operation Overlord. *Photo Superstock.* HAMM, LUXEMBOURG—U.S. military cemetery, where over 6,000 soldiers of the 3rd Army lie, one of which is General George S. Patton. *Photo Farrell Grehan/FPG International.*

In Flanders Fields the poppies blow
Between the crosses, row on row,
That mark our place; and in the sky
The larks, still bravely singing, fly
Scarce heard amid the guns below.

To you from failing hands we throw
The torch; be yours to hold it high.
If ye break faith with us who die
We shall not sleep, though poppies grow
In Flanders Fields.

John McCrae

Eternal Father, strong to save,
Whose arm hath bound the restless wave,
Who bidd'st the mighty ocean deep
Its own appointed limits keep,
O hear us when we cry to Thee
For those in peril on the sea!

O Christ! whose voice the waters heard
And hushed their raging at Thy word,
Who walkedst on the foaming deep
And calm amidst its rage didst sleep,
O hear us when we cry to Thee
For those in peril on the sea!

Most Holy Spirit! who didst brood
Upon the chaos dark and rude
And bid its angry tumult cease
And give, for wild confusion, peace,
O hear us when we cry to Thee
For those in peril on the sea!

William Whiting
Navy Hymn